HUMAN RIGHTS
IN THE WORLD

HUMAN RIGHTS
IN THE WORLD

*A Report to the
European Parliament*

presented by

KEN COATES MEP

SPOKESMAN

First published in Great Britain in 1992 by
Spokesman
Bertrand Russell House
Gamble Street
Nottingham, England
Tel. 0602 708318

British Library Cataloguing in Publication Data available on request.

ISBN 0-85124-542-0 cloth
ISBN 0-85124-543-9 paper

Printed by the Russell Press Ltd, Nottingham
(Tel. 0602 784505)

Contents

Preface 1

Part I
Explanatory Statement 7
  Annus Mirabilis of 1989 8
  Europe in the World 9
  Human Rights in the European Community 12
  Immigration, Population Movement and Racism 15
  Minorities and Indigenous Peoples 22
  Positive and Negative Human Rights Developments in
    Third Countries 26
  Progress towards Democracy 27
  Conflict Resolution 36
  Human Rights of Children 38
  Regional Human Rights Systems 43
  African, Caribbean and Pacific Countries 46
  The United Nations Human Rights System 48
  The Role of the European Parliament and
    Community Policy 53

Part II
  Resolution 63

Preface

In 1991, I presented the report on Human Rights in the World to the European Parliament. This is what I said.

'We live in hope, Mr President.

It is two centuries since the great American Revolutionary, Tom Paine, was forced to run from England to France because he had dared, in 1791, to publish *The Rights of Man*. The first book of this tract for the times concludes with the then immense hope that:

> ...the intrigue of Courts, by which the system of war is kept up, may provoke a confederation of Nations to abolish it: and a European Congress, to patronise the progress of free Government...

Now, today, just such a Congress is assembled here to give its considered judgement on the state of human rights in the world. In presenting my report, I must first register my profound thanks to colleagues of all parties who have worked with enthusiasm and a complete lack of rancour towards agreement on what it proposes. Similar thanks are due to members of our very small and overworked staff, especially Mr Barry Waters.

The report covers events in the years 1989 and 1990. It registers a considerable growth in the recognition of human rights, and it is particularly concerned to welcome the extension of pluralist democratic norms to so many territories in Central and Eastern Europe. In Latin America and parts of Africa there has also been important progress of this kind. Of course, our report presumes a strong correlation between democratic institutions and the observance of human rights, even if, notwithstanding the good advice of Tom Paine, the fit between the two remains far from perfect. The report reaffirms and builds upon the good work done by its predecessors.

At the same time, it records vast areas of problems and injustice. Wars and sharp political crises still displace millions of people from their homes.

The world has 15 million refugees and 20 million other displaced persons. The European contribution to meeting this tragedy is far from adequate, and the main burdens fall on some of the poorest countries.

The 1990 World Summit for Children brought home to us the existence of an immense distress, with 15 million child deaths each year, 100 million child slaves, and widespread imprisonment, torture and murder of children in the course of civil conflicts. Oceans of such child abuse surround us, and will guarantee new traumas as these suffering new generations mature.

The report is much concerned with the wide scale of torture. It has to draw attention to the continued operation of 'death squads'. A separate report will document the extent and limits of progress in ending the death penalty, but some of the bare facts are here outlined. They will encourage no one.

Very large numbers of executions have taken place in Iran, Iraq and China, and many other countries have put people to death without giving them any proper trial. A ruling in the Supreme Court in 1989 allows the execution of juvenile offenders and mentally retarded people in the USA, much to our surprise and disquiet.

The report also considers the conditions of indigenous peoples, threatened by the encroachment of economic exploitation in their regions, and examines the very serious increase in ethnic and intercommunal conflicts around the world.

We have already debated the dreadful events in Yugoslavia, which serve to illustrate the lethal effects of such explosions.

With the widening spread of information, however, these matters do become well known throughout the world. The knowledge thus diffused stimulates a welcome growth in human rights movements, and in official responses to the initiatives of non-governmental organisations.

The report is able to draw support from the growth of regional systems of human rights protection, whose examples become richer. Together with the European Community, the countries associated in the Lomé IV agreement will be able to respond to, and reinforce, the upholding of rights. And yet the closure of East-West conflict has made more apparent to everyone the implications of global polarisation of the North-South axis, which is an axis of hunger and indebtedness. A very large part of the human rights agenda today stems directly from this polarity. Human rights will only become really universal when each of us can be, and not simply proclaim that we are, our brothers', and our sisters', keeper.

To this end, Mr President, the report makes a series of two dozen specific proposals about Community policy; several about relations with, and between, the United Nations and its agencies, and some about the activities of Parliament itself.

Not the least of these is paragraph 63 which, if it is accepted, resolves that Parliament should will the means to engage itself, with optimum efficiency, to achieve the goals upon which it is, I am sure, quite ready to agree.

Two hundred years ago, Tom Paine's great appeal was banned, and even burned, in Britain. But, after half a century, it was read more widely than any other democratic writing by the Chartists, who sought the universal suffrage.

The people of the world still live in hope.

Nowadays, I was informed by the Dalai Lama, clandestine editions of the Universal Declaration of Human Rights are passed from hand to hand in Tibet.

We shall have to do our duty, sharing our concern and others' hopes, if human rights are to reach across the world, excluding none and embracing all.'

Ken Coates MEP

PART I

Human Rights in the World

Explanatory Statement

The custom of drawing up an 'annual' report on 'human rights in the world and Community human rights policy' was initiated by the Political Affairs Committee during the first legislature of the directly elected Parliament. Since 1983 five 'annual' reports have been drawn up. In effect each 'annual' report has covered a span of more than twelve months and this is also the case with the present report which, because of the intervention of the 1989 elections, will cover the years 1989 and 1990. The previous report, presented by Mr de Gucht, was adopted by Parliament in February 1989. Thus, this year the word 'annual' has been dropped from the title of the report, and it is proposed that this should be the case in future — until such time as the rhythm of committee work and the provision of additional resources do indeed permit an 'annual' report to be produced every twelve months.

It may be worth recalling that the original idea of the Political Affairs Committee's Working Group on Human Rights (which preceded the Human Rights Subcommittee) was that an annual report should be submitted to Parliament by Council/European Political Cooperation in the same way that the US Department of State reports to Congress every year. Council, however, indicated that it was neither willing nor able to come forward with such a text, and Parliament decided in 1981 that it would itself compile an 'annual report'.

This text has never sought to match the annual reports produced by the Department of State, by Amnesty International, by the Frankfurter *Gesellschaft für Menschenrechte* and by other bodies. Up to now, Parliament has not equipped itself with the resources for such a task; and there would be little sense in duplicating the work of other organisations.

Parliament, however, is in a unique position to engage itself in the human rights field, and our experience shows that its intervention can be highly effective. Up to now its report has sought to serve as a compilation of Community activity in the field of human rights, to reflect on the significance of major developments in the world with regard to human rights and on the Community's reaction to such events, and to indicate how the Community and the European Parliament might be evolving a more comprehensive (and effective) policy on human rights. The present report will be no exception.

Annus Mirabilis of 1989

As the accompanying resolution indicates, it was widely believed that events in the period under review gave more grounds for optimism about progress in the field of human rights than in earlier years. Much of this optimism, of course, stemmed from the dramatic changes which swept through Central and Eastern Europe in 1989, making that year, arguably that of the most significant peaceful political change in recent history, with far-reaching worldwide effects. Indeed, so far as the European Community is concerned, it could be said that the year 1989 overtook the year 1992, at least with regard to its political consequences.

Parliament has repeatedly expressed the belief that we can best promote human rights by seeking to extend democratic pluralistic political systems as widely as possible. Of course, these systems may well be imperfect, perhaps even badly flawed. Nonetheless, experience does show that fundamental human rights flourish most easily in such political soil. Unfortunately, those who enjoy such rights are not always enthusiastic about sharing them with others who may live in less hospitable terrains.

It should be mentioned here that Parliament, in its 'annual' reports has always, since its first report in 1983, given particular emphasis to three fundamental rights — the right to life, the right to respect for the physical and moral integrity of the person, and the right to a fair trial by an independent court. Parliament has thus stressed what might be termed 'natural' or 'inalienable' rights, reflecting a tradition of political thinking which can be traced back in modern times to such political philosophers as Locke, Montesquieu and Hume. It was Locke who affirmed that the end of government is the preservation of liberty; and that this could best be achieved by means of a system of checks and balances which prevented tyrannous or dictatorial regimes from abrogating the civil and political rights of citizens, which it was the duty of the state to protect.

At the same time, however, as according primacy to certain fundamental rights, Parliament has always recognised that all human rights are indivisible and intertwined. The Community has no less an obligation to seek to enhance economic, social and cultural rights than it has to promote the protection of 'classic' political and civil rights. It is for this reason that a significant part of this report always has been the opinion of Parliament's Development Committee which has invariably emphasised the need to pay heed also to other rights. As put recently by a colleague in a debate in the Political Affairs Committee: 'Surely the right to water is an inalienable right'. Your rapporteur takes the view that the 'right to water' is comprised in the right to life, but he also believes it to be undeniable that conditions of life are significant in permitting a society to enjoy the rights to which all human beings are entitled.

This raises the question of what constitutes a 'human right'. This has been a regular matter for debate since the Working Group was established in 1980. It would be fair to say that the 'right' to conscientious objection, or to development, or to 'adequate housing' would still be considered as 'goals' rather than rights by a significant segment of opinion within the Political Affairs Committee, despite recognition of both as fundamental rights in some internationally accepted conventions and declarations. This kind of debate, however, is somewhat academic in view of the Political Affairs Committee's competences and decision to focus primarily in its initiatives and in reports such as this on certain rights universally accepted as 'fundamental'. Put more concretely, it might be said that the consensual view in the Subcommitee is that although governments may not always be in a position to enhance the well-being of their citizens, they can prevent their agents from torturing their citizens.

Europe in the World

It is particularly important, in view of the significance for Europe of the events of 1989, that sight is not lost of the general world context in which respect for human rights is evolving. At the same time as we talk about one Europe from the Atlantic to the Urals, we must remain conscious that the family of mankind all inhabits one globe. Although the developed world, in general, continues to make positive economic and social progress, the gap between the developed world and the developing world is growing ever greater. Economic transfers from the South to the North amount today to the equivalent of several Marshall Plans in reverse. Even within our own societies there would appear in some countries to be more economic and social divergence than convergence. Without wishing to sound Malthusian, it must be recognised that population growth is again legitimately giving considerable cause for alarm, and that one effect of this is likely to be to exacerbate further such divergences. Poor populations grow quicker than rich ones, but the behaviour of the rich frequently aggravates the poverty which surrounds them.

The statistics for world debt speak for themselves as an indicator of the imbalances which exist in the world, an issue which it is now clearly perceived is not merely a matter of economics, but also a political and moral issue. (This problem is being examined in a report being drawn up for the Political Affairs Committee by Mr Claude Cheysson and is also to be the subject of a public hearing by the Committee, together with the Committee on Development and Cooperation). In short, there is arguably more human deprivation in the world today than at any time in the recent past. Figures for worldwide population displacements and refugees, for instance, are at their highest levels for many years. So while focusing on respect for the 'classic' political and civil rights, we should not lose sight of the circumstances in which they have been exercised. These circumstances may be jeopardised, and will indeed be jeopardised if global poverty continues to grow.

If certain human rights are suppressed by governments which exercise real choices, about whether to behave in a more or less enlightened manner, it remains true that economic hardship may powerfully narrow those areas of choice. Debt and poverty may promote turbulence and impose adverse changes which might never have been considered in times of greater affluence. If it is true that the framework of pluralism may be very difficult to maintain in periods of acute economic hardship, how much more difficult is the establishment of such a democratic framework on the ruins of dictatorship, in such a regime of adversity? The democratic experiments in both Latin America and Eastern Europe frequently involve states which are heavily in debt. That their debts were incurred by former autocrats makes them no easier to bear. Tom Paine once claimed that no one generation has the right to bind the next. His words would not be welcomed by the lenders who seek to recoup their losses in the world-wide crisis of indebtedness which confronts us all today.

It is worth recalling the words of Czech President Vaclav Havel in his address to the US Congress in March 1990:

'Without a global revolution in the sphere of human consciousness, nothing will change for the better in the sphere of our being as humans, and the catastrophe toward which this world is headed — be it ecological, social, demographic or a general breakdown of civilisation — will be unavoidable. If we are no longer threatened by world war or by the danger that the absurd mountains of accumulated nuclear weapons might blow up the world, this does not mean that we have definitely won'.

This seems to be a more realistic way of viewing the situation on our planet than that attributed to Mr Francis Fukuyama, the former United States State Department official, who saw in the events of 1989 'the end of history' Mr Fukuyama claims that he has been widely misunderstood. The claim that the collapse of centralised Communist States, and the resultant resurgence of liberal and capitalist thought, implies the beginning of a new age seems to draw large conclusions from relatively small evidence. Consumer capitalism is very far from establishing itself in triumph throughout Eastern Europe and the Soviet Union. True, its lack there is much bemoaned and there are now many people who would be happy if they could simply change their economic system. To change from a badly planned economy to an efficient and advanced market system is not possible without great pain. It also needs skill and luck beyond normal expectations. It might be easier to transform a backward planned economy into a backward and inefficient market.

At the moment, though, there seems to be almost as much ideology in today's expectations of 'the market' as there was yesterday in celebrations of 'the plan'. Markets are good for some things, and plans are good for others. Far from simply embodying free markets, today's great corporations have developed forms of planning which are both rigorous and comprehensive. Like other plans, they may sometimes harm the people they affect, and they frequently damage the environment. One-sided hymns to the market on one side or the plan on the other quickly become unrealistic, and may remind us of the cargo cults which swept across Papua New Guinea and other Southern Pacific islands during the post-war years.

Noticing that the missionaries were happy, the indigenous inhabitants of Papua attributed this ophelimity to the regular arrival of supplies of gin in friendly aeroplanes. Not wishing to be left behind, they mobilised their own peoples to level large airstrips in the hills, and kindle great fires to light the pilots in with their precious cargoes. No planes, however, came. Sometimes we may think that the invocation of the market in Eastern Europe is similarly hopeful. Unfortunately, it may be that the airmen will actually come in answer to the beckoning flares, only to carry away the little quantities of gin already belonging to the natives there.

Ideology apart, we are bound to observe that in Central and Eastern Europe, the 'end of history' notwithstanding, the potential for political convulsions would appear to be as great as ever. The turbulence already being caused by renascent nationalisms and ethnic consciousness will provide at least one challenge which will not be placated by market economics alone. Will it, indeed, remain compatible with pluralist democracy? Does not democracy require a strong and stable framework on which to grow and flourish?

The European Community, if it remains the core of a new 'concentric circles' Europe, can seek to influence these changes for the better. We might even extend the concept of concentric circles to Asia and Africa, not in a hegemonic fashion but in recognition of our linkages, and our geographical proximity and interdependence. The invasion of Kuwait by Iraq has again shown only too clearly how events in one corner of the world can affect us all. Shall we draw the conclusion that economic and monetary union can lead us outwards to a new and redistributive global economic order? If we choose, instead, fortress Europe, will we not stoke up new furnaces in large areas of the world?

It could be seen as positive that we are now in a position to openly seek to help resolve some of the tensions in Central and Eastern Europe, many of which have been suffocated for decades by authoritarian regimes. A few months ago, many would have said, 'turbulent as the situation in the Soviet Union may be in the years ahead, this must surely be more welcome than the traumas which were seen in Tiananmen Square in June 1989'. Optimism is rarer now, but does it lead us to deny that, the more openhanded and the less restrictive our help can be, the more positive it will be?

Human Rights in the European Community

In looking outward at the world one should not forget that the reforms and changes taking place in Moscow and elsewhere will also lead us to re-examine some of the values of our own societies in Western Europe. (It is perhaps no coincidence that the argument for a Bill of Rights in Great Britain should have come into such prominence during the past three years. The 'Charter 88' movement reflects misgivings about the British Constitution, whose weaknesses have become more and more evident at a time of single-minded radical reform. An alternative remedy to national constitutional inadequacies is, of course, the establishment of an appropriate net of safeguards at European level, and it is interesting to see this argument taking shape.)

However, the focus of this report is human rights in countries outside the European Community. In the European Parliament the competence of the Political Affairs Committee and its Subcommittee on Human Rights has been the protection of human rights in third countries since it was deemed that, within the Community, these matters can be raised within the established legal framework which is subject to scrutiny by the European Parliament. Where third countries were concerned, no such formal possibilities for effective action through the legal system existed. Hence the division of competences between the Political Affairs Committee and the Committee on Legal Affairs and Citizens Rights, which, together with the Committee on Petitions, is responsible for human rights within the Community.

Your rapporteur, while recognising that this division of competences does have certain practical advantages (for instance the Political Affairs Committee's direct link to European Political Cooperation, which is a principal channel for expressing Community human rights concerns in third countries), is doubtful about the wisdom of this. It should be noted too that although the European Parliament has not made any significant changes to its committee competences with regard to human rights since 1979, it has voted in the two previous annual reports that human rights both within and outside the Community should fall to the competence of the same committee.

Let us look at a relevant concrete example. Since the European Parliament elections in 1989 the Subcommittee on Human Rights has sought to develop an institutionalised dialogue on human rights problems with its parliamentary counterparts in the Soviet Union and Turkey. It has been clear from the outset that this must imply the development of reciprocal exchanges. Having secured the release of some would-be Jewish emigrants as a result of the good offices of the Chairman of the Supreme Soviet Subcommittee on Humanitarian and Cultural Affairs, Mr Burlatsky, we would be naive if we did not anticipate some requests coming in the opposite direction. That the Parliament itself has been deeply concerned about particular cases which have arisen inside our Community does not adequately answer this problem. Lacking the competence to reply directly on such matters, your Subcommittee would have to inform its partners in dialogue that their responses should come from another Committee. This is hardly the most efficient way to improve the framework of international exchanges.

The author of the previous annual report, Mr de Gucht, focused in some detail on the blurring of the distinction between consideration of human rights matters within and outside the Community, and also on the overlap and lacunae in human rights protection within the Community itself.

Everything signalled in that report remains valid. Indeed reflections of this kind may be even more relevant today. There is for instance the prospect that the newly evolving CSCE mechanisms and instruments to which EC Member countries will subscribe could run parallel to or overlap with similar provisions to which we are bound as signatories to the European Convention on Human Rights.

Within the Community itself, there is currently much debate about more advanced forms of protection of human rights. Such matters were explored in some depth at a series of conferences organised by the European University of Florence under the auspices of the European Commission and Parliament on: 'Human Rights and the European Community: Towards 1992 and beyond'. Conceived as an initiative to commemorate the bicentennial of the 1789 Declaration of the Rights of Man in France, it had by the final conference in Strasbourg on 20-21 November 1989 led to the conception of a thought-provoking agenda and an impressive compilation of studies on the problems confronting the Europe of today and tomorrow with regard to human rights.

Your rapporteur believes that these concerns remain particularly relevant at the time of the two intergovernmental conferences and in the run-up to 1992. The former may provide an opportunity to make up for the absence of a Community 'bill of rights' in the founding treaties which is being increasingly perceived as something of a lacuna in the Community's 'constitution'.

Relevant here is the recommendation in the resolution[1] adopted by Parliament in July 1990, and drawn up for the Institutional Committee by Mr David Martin. It states in paragraph 18:

> 'Calls for the incorporation into the Treaties of the declaration of fundamental rights and freedoms approved by the European Parliament on 12 April 1989; calls for the incorporation into the Treaties of the Declaration against racism and xenophobia adopted by Parliament on 11 June 1986; calls for the Court of Justice to have jurisdiction for the protection of these fundamental rights vis-à-vis the Community with the possibility of direct access to the Court of Justice for Community citizens after national appeal procedures have been exhausted; considers furthermore that the Community should accede to the European Convention on Human Rights of the Council of Europe in order for the Community's procedures protecting fundamental rights to be subject to appeal to an external body at least in the areas covered by the Convention (in the same way as individual States, even those with charters of rights of their own, are subject to the European Convention)'.

It is nevertheless true that the Court of Justice, basing itself on the provisions in Member States' constitutions and international agreements such as the European Convention, has stated that it will use these provisions to protect fundamental human rights which might be threatened by Community legislation or decisions. This was further affirmed in the preamble to the Single European Act. Furthermore, over the years, there has been a degree of highly necessary internal legislative consolidation. This development has underpinned and to some extent justified the Community's evolving human rights perspective in its external relations. If there was a domestic Community face of human rights, then, *ipso facto*, this also had to be represented in its relations with third countries.

Indeed, the initial justification for human rights work by the Community in third countries stems from the Community's legal framework and from the political beliefs which led to the Community's establishment. The Community was the coming together of democratic nations under law, with the protection of citizens' rights a cardinal aspect of its identity. Thus, from the outset, it could be argued that the Community had an implicit duty to prevent the undermining of the values it represented by conniving at inhumanity outside its territories — even though this function was not set out in writing in the founding Treaties.

'Europe' is often thought to be less than modest in its pretensions concerning human rights. Nevertheless, there is no other corner of the globe in which an individual citizen has to anything like the same extent the possibility of seeking and obtaining judicial remedies against his own government from a higher regional, i.e. European, body. Where changes have taken place in Eastern Europe, has this not been partly due to the example of Western Europe in the post-war years? How far did the growth of civil societies in the West give countries in Eastern Europe the hope that similar societies could be created in their own countries? Are the citizens of Eastern and Central Europe turning toward Western Europe only because goods of greater quality and abundance are available there, or are they attracted also because our societies, individually and collectively, have managed to create a political and civil environment in which the rights of the individual are better respected?

We cannot afford to be complacent about these matters. The only way in which we can ensure that the legal perversities and injustices in our societies are kept to a minimum is by constant vigilance, and by a constant struggle to improve the standards which we set ourselves (but do not always manage to respect). We shall doubtless be observing such a struggle in a very acute form in Eastern and Central Europe as the legislation of their new civil order is put in place and their citizens lay claim to the means to protect, promote and guarantee their own fundamental rights.

Immigration, Population Movement and Racism

In his report, Mr de Gucht indicated a number of issues where the distinction intra-Community/extra-Community had become blurred and how the European Community appeared to be increasingly open to charges of hypocrisy or of applying double standards. One issue which he did not mention is immigration. In the context of current demographic changes, your rapporteur believes that policy in this regard and its application is one of the touchstones of European human rights policy, obliging us to examine in the same optic the situation in third countries and in the Community itself.

There is no question that one of the most burning political and social issues in a number of Community countries today concerns the treatment of migrant communities. Racist and xenophobic attitudes have undoubtedly stimulated the rise of the 'New Right' in Western Europe. In response to this phenomenon Parliament in September 1984 established its own Committee of Inquiry into Racism and Xenophobia, which led to the adoption of the 'Evrigenis'[2] report and the Joint Declaration on racism and xenophobia of June 1986.[3] More recently a follow-up Committee of Inquiry with a similar remit worked over a period of nine months to adopt the 'Ford' report,[4] which formed the basis of a debate in plenary in October 1990, where two resolutions on the report by the Committee of Inquiry into Racism and Xenophobia[5] were adopted.

Parliament has consistently taken a progressive position on all such issues. In June 1990, for instance, a resolution of Parliament expressed indignation that the Council, in its resolution on the fight against racism and xenophobia within the Community does not take immigrants from third countries into account. It considered that this failing went against the spirit of the Joint Declaration and decided to examine further the legal possibilities of an appeal against the Council. At the same part-session Parliament also adopted three reports on the right of residence in the Community and called for the establishment of a true 'right of residence' (with the institution of a European Resident's Card) for all Community citizens and second generation immigrants as well as for recognised political refugees and stateless persons. It should be said, however, that many paragraphs of the above-mentioned resolutions were adopted by narrow majorities, reflecting a significant division of views on these issues. Again your rapporteur would stress the importance of viewing these matters in a world perspective. We must recognise, for instance, that in a world where numbers of refugees and displaced persons are at their highest in decades, Europe is no longer a *Terre d'Asile* of great significance. This situation may change with the prospect of very significant population movement from Eastern Europe in the coming years.

Nevertheless, in the European Community, as in Eastern and Central Europe, there has been a rise in anti-Semitic feeling and against established ethnic minorities, as well as against sections of the 8 million non-EC citizens legally resident in the Community. Of greater concern to governments are the illegal economic migrants in the European Community for which a variety of estimates exist (ranging from 4 to 6 million). Their exploitation and generally abysmal living conditions are reported to have led the Commission of the European Community to carry out an unpublished study in 1989 which concluded that the destabilising phenomenon of illegal immigration would get even more out of control in the years to come — particularly the migration to Mediterranean Europe from South Asia, the Near East and North Africa.

The Human Rights Subcommittee and Political Affairs Committee did seek at the start of this legislature to draw up a report on the matter of clandestine immigration. This was, however, refused by the Bureau of Parliament which instead authorised the European Parliament's Legal Affairs Committee to draw up a report on the free circulation of persons and the problems of internal security within the Community[6] to which the Political Affairs Committee is to give an opinion.

Clandestine immigration has been seen particularly in the context of the 1992 programme, with certain countries taking the view that 'a Europe without frontiers' would make this problem harder to control. Some of Parliament's concerns have been made very clear in resolutions on the Schengen Agreement and on the Convention signed in June 1990 by the Justice and/or Interior Ministers of the Twelve (except for Denmark) to establish which state would be responsible for reviewing an asylum application filed in the Europe without frontiers of 1993. Parliament has been criticial of both agreements on the grounds that the negotiations were conducted without any public or parliamentary scrutiny. Parliament considered that the content in the Convention on right of asylum presents risks for individual freedoms. It called on the five Schengen countries not to sign the additional protocol as long as it was not guaranteed that Interpol would be fully excluded from the computerised exchange system. Parliament called on the intergovernmental conference to include in the Community's exclusive competence the problems of entry, movement and residence of third country nationals, as well as the issues of terrorism, criminality, drug trafficking and illicit trade in works of art and antiques. It urged that the Commission be allowed to take part in the work of the intergovernmental 'ad hoc immigration group' ('The Trevi Group') in its capacity as the Community institution whose mission is to be the guardian of the Treaties. A particular concern is that a clear distinction be made between the treatment of refugees and asylum seekers on the one hand, and suspected terrorists and criminals on the other.

With regard to the above issues, Parliament has consistently taken the view that in the perspective of 1992 and a united Europe, there must be common Community positions, based on the treaties, and not on inter-governmental Conventions or agreements signed between the Member States. In this perspective it has decided to organise in June 1991 a European conference on migrant workers from third countries in order to seek a common approach to the issue and to stimulate overall and coordinated Community action.

In addition to the significant migration from third countries principally to the Mediterranean countries of the Community, major population movement, (particularly to West Germany), as a result of the events in Eastern Europe, has made the question of migration particularly topical. The debate which this has triggered obliges us to consider the extent to which in a 'concentric circles' Europe the circles will be related and to what extent passage will be possible from the outer to the inner rings. The political developments in the USSR and elsewhere have obliged us to consider as a matter of priority the problem of nationality, ethnic and group rights, as well as resurgent racism and xenophobia in Eastern Europe typified by such phenomena as the rise of *Pamyat* and the persecution of gypsies.

It was significant that at the CSCE 'human dimension' conference in June 1990 in Copenhagen the issue of minorities was one of the hardest on which to reach a consensus in the concluding document.

Thus, for the European Community and the European Parliament to see refugee and asylum problems as principally an extra-Community problem is no longer possible. One topical example is the movement of 'East' Germans to what was 'West' Germany, which is in turn exerting pressure on established Turkish or Yugoslav communities to return to their countries of origin.

Another relevant example in this connection might be the question of human rights in Hong Kong now and after the proposed handover in 1997. There is a clear Community dimension to this problem, since decisions to grant residency status to Hong Kong citizens in the UK would also eventually give them the possibility of residing elsewhere in the Community — as would the inhabitants of Macau, all of whom have the right to Portuguese citizenship. (A report on this issue is currently being drawn up by Mr Bertens on behalf of the Subcommittee and the Political Affairs Committee.)

Such examples underline the necessity for the European Community to formulate and apply policies which are seen to be consistent if it is to retain moral credibility as a Community. It cannot condemn the situation in camps for 'boat people' in Hong Kong, or the policies of the UK government on repatriation to Vietnam, or the 'push-back' policies which have been applied on occasion in Thailand unless it is willing to accept its share of the refugee burden and all that it implies.

In December 1989 the European Parliament called on the British government to abandon its policy of forced repatriation of boat people from Hong Kong to Vietnam. But it must be said there is no clear Community policy or view with regard to how this problem should be resolved. Parliament also has stated that human rights have been violated in expulsions and in the procedures at airports in various European countries.

It would certainly appear a matter of urgency to establish a common Community system of scrutiny, a common policy on political refugees, and perhaps the adherence of the Community as a whole to the UN Convention on the status of refugees. The European Parliament and the Community must do everything possible to ensure that the move to a single market by the end of 1992 will not be at the expense of the rights of immigrants and political refugees.

All of the above does argue that human rights should be made an element of the Community's 'written constitution' and this should be considered at the inter-governmental conference. Previous rapporteurs have called for the Community to endow itself with an explicit and specific legal mandate concerning its competences in the field of human rights, suggesting that on the basis of Article 235 an appropriate form of 'Community Act' could be adopted. Your rapporteur believes Parliament must now press for this aim to be achieved through the inter-governmental conference.

But issues such as migration must be addressed not just at the Community level but between the Community and the wider Europe — whether it is the 23 of the Council of Europe or the 35 of the CSCE. For instance, since 1987, the Council of Europe has been running a coordinated multidisciplinary project on inter-community (i.e. migrant-host population) relations to improve links and make for better understanding between the various groups. European Community Ministers responsible for migratory issues met in Oporto (Portugal) in May 1987 and stressed their support for a policy of international relations applied coherently to every sector of society. There was concern to enlist help of the media and the education system to back migrants' right to respect for their cultural identity, to bring the EC to the threshold of a multicultural 1992. The proposed establishment by the European Community of a 'Migrants Forum' would provide a focus and a natural interlocutor for the Community institutions. The European Parliament, in this spirit, voted on 15 March 1989 for European Community 'foreigners' to be given the right to vote in local elections.

It is clear that the European Community must go much further as a Community on such issues. Procedures for receiving and integrating migrants vary from country to country. Very often it is community groups and voluntary agencies which try to provide services to meet the special needs of newcomers. In a Europe without frontiers European Community countries must surely be able profitably to pool their experiences. The 'European' dimension is appropriate because it would bring pressure to bear on those European Community governments whose procedures may not be consistent with international refugee law. This is not to suggest that the European Community or the Council of Europe should usurp the role of the United Nations High Commission for Refugees, which for instance has encouraged governments to adapt their procedures; in the UK, for example, since 1988 almost all asylum seekers at ports of entry are referred to the UNHCR or UKIAS (UK Immigrants' Advisory Service) for legal representation. Nevertheless, the European Parliament has consistently argued for regional methods of problem solving; and if we view the issue of migration to Europe as a regional European problem, it might seem appropriate that we devise our own common mechanisms.

What is certain is that international conventions and treaties are one thing — an indispensable normative activity. But to ensure that the standards set are implemented and respected, and that there is on-the-ground follow-through and support, is quite another. That is why in the past the Human Rights Subcommittee has stressed the need in European Community budgetary allocations for human rights projects to go less to research studies and be targeted more to specific grass-roots projects.[7]

Some might consider the foregoing comments as exceeding the competence of the Human Rights Subcommittee and the Political Affairs Committee. Your rapporteur's purpose was to indicate that with regard to certain pressing human rights issues, it is no longer possible to make such clear divisions between what is intra-Community and what is extra-Community. Another example might be the incendiary furore over Salman Rushdie and his novel *The Satanic Verses* which sparked in return more intolerance, fear and resentment. Fundamentalism and moves to an integrated Islam expressed outside the European Community confirmed in many Europeans' minds the stereotype of Islam as a religion of intolerance and violence which would then in turn stereotype the approximately 7 million Moslems in Western Europe. This has been further exacerbated by the Gulf crisis. This does not augur well for the wider acceptance and enfranchisement of Muslims in Europe. Like all great religions, Islam contains within itself different possibilities, and it is imprudent as well as unfair to impose a restrictive view of these upon ourselves.

Despite the tensions engendered by such issues, and despite public perceptions, Europe is not in fact 'bearing the brunt' of a worldwide refugee problem. The world today has some 12 to 15 million refugees, compared with 4.6 million a decade ago, with the numbers having increased since our last annual report. If you add in all categories of displaced persons, the numbers are significantly higher. Most are either criss-crossing borders, fleeing war and drought in various countries, desperately seeking food and sanctuary, or in vast refugee camps, as in Bangladesh, Thailand, Mexico, Honduras, Sudan, Zambia, Malawi and Hong Kong. The situation would appear to be most dire in Sub-Saharan Africa, with one-tenth of the world's population, which now accounts for about a third of the world's officially recognised refugees. The region also has about 12 million displaced persons.[8]

Public opinion in potential host countries varies greatly. And for these countries the dilemma referred to earlier remains: how can refugees' legitimate need for sanctuary be reconciled with nations' desire to control their borders? There can be no question that the richer nations should share the burden more fairly. Although the situation has changed since Europe opened up to the East, West European countries and Japan have been far less generous than, for instance, the US and Canada in accepting third world refugees.

The burden could certainly be eased if political and economic stability could be brought to affected regions — in Central America or the Horn of Africa for instance. Much thinking in Europe favours regional solutions with Southeast Asian countries like Malaysia and Thailand accepting more refugees for long-term resettlement. Nevertheless, this cannot permit the European Community to duck the issue. It is now more than ever necessary for the European Community to participate more fully in the work of the UNHCR, as an observer, to decide together on 'burden-sharing' and to devise a European mechanism (in the optic of 1992) to harmonise and control police procedures for reception of refugees and to humanise the variety of 'deterrent' legal measures in the European Community, which, despite international norms, vary enormously?

It has been suggested, for instance, that the European Parliament might envisage drawing up a charter for refugees to prompt Community action, going beyond the current situation of inter-governmental meetings to harmonise (downwards) their asylum policies. As indicated earlier, in some European countries, compared with, say, Canada, there is no infrastructure to deal with refugees. It must also be said, however, that measures to stem the illegal flow of immigrants, whether it be across the Rio Grande or into parts of Southern Europe, are equally harsh, and insofar as many of the above are economic refugees and law-breakers, are deemed by some to be justified. Such 'justification', to carry any conviction at all, would depend upon serious efforts to ameliorate the economic pressures which generate population movements in the first place. Should we perhaps look to a coherent European Community resettlement programme along the lines of that of the United States, based on the Refugee Act of 1980, and, more recently, in Canada? The fact remains that the so-called 'irregular movements' of population are no longer a temporary blip on the screen but a long-term problem. Your rapporteur would not wish here to enter the complex debate about economic migrants and political refugees. But such issues will undoubtedly be very much with us in the years to come. When Mr Burlatsky addressed the Political Affairs Committee in October 1990, he mentioned that the liberalisation of Soviet laws on freedom of migration might result in a movement of several million people Westwards. Since we in the West consistently advocated such liberalisation, how do we propose to cope with its effects? Do we intend to build a wall?

Minorities and Indigenous Peoples

Another worldwide human rights problem, on which the Community should be forming a view, based on its own experience, concerns the situation and rights of minorities and indigenous peoples. This, also, is an example of an issue where it is not helpful to distinguish between human rights within and outside the Community. It may be argued that it is incorrect to examine the problems of 'minorities' and 'indigenous peoples' together. There is, however, considerable overlap in the problems posed. Such issues, and further thinking about 'the right of self-determination' have come very much to the fore as a result of the changes in Central and Eastern Europe, which have highlighted the extent to which conflicts in the world stem from tension between majority and minority groups.

It seems appropriate to recall here that 1992, as well as being a landmark year for the construction of Europe, also marks the 500th anniversary of the discovery of America by Columbus. With this in mind, the United Nations General Assembly has declared that 1993 should be designated as the 'International Year for Indigenous Rights'. (1992 was originally the year proposed by the Working

Group on Indigenous Populations. But, at the request of Spain, the Commission on Human Rights called only for an International year, not specifying 1992.)

The UN Sub-Commission also has called for the organisation during 1991 of a 'technical conference' on practical experience in the realisation of sustainable and environmentally sound self-development of indigenous peoples with the participation of experts from governments, appropriate specialised agencies and indigenous peoples' organisations.

Shortly after the previous annual report was adopted, the Political Affairs Committee, using procedure without plenary debate, adopted a report (presented by Mrs van den Heuvel) on the 'Situation of Indians in the world'. This, in effect, focused on the situation of Amer-Indians. In the past two years there has been even more public sensitivity to their situation, partly stemming from concerns about the destruction of the South American rain forest, partly because of certain much-publicised legal battles such as between the Mohawks and the government of Canada, and between Hopi and Navajo in Arizona, and partly as a result of a growing recognition that in Latin America, despite the political progress being made, the Indians remain, more than ever, the most marginalised social group, including those in countries (Peru, Bolivia and Guatemala) where they make up a majority of the population.

In the past, when the question of indigenous peoples has arisen, it is to the Americas that attention has invariably turned, since the American Indians are clearly definable indigenous peoples and generally accepted as such. In Asia and Africa it always has been far more difficult to define an 'indigenous group'; but world attention has now also turned very much in that direction as a result of the changes in Europe and Asia and the resurgence of ethnic consciousness.

These issues were more than touched on during a public hearing organised by the Political Affairs Committee in April 1990 on Tibet. An impressive body of evidence was heard, and a report on this subject is now being drawn up. One may dispute whether Tibetans constitute an indigenous people, but it would seem fair to state that a distinct ethnic culture is being undermined by the People's Republic of China. Repression, which is a matter of conscious public policy, is only part of the problem. Economic decisions which may not have been designed to imperil the indigenous peoples, can have an even more lethal effect upon their survival.

Considering the rights of indigenous peoples, like problems of migration, is something which is not readily attempted in a world where national sovereignty is an essential feature of international relations. Paradoxically, however, it is at the UN, which exemplifies the preeminence of the nation state, that perhaps the most passionate debate on these issues has been generated. In May 1982 the Sub-Commission on Prevention of Discrimination and Protection of Minorities established a 'Working Group on Indigenous Populations'. This provided, for the first time, a significant international forum where representatives of indigenous groups could air their views, and also participate in drafting standards for their protection. Elsewhere in the UN system the right to speak is generally limited to states, intergovernmental agencies and accredited non-governmental organisations (NGOs). The meetings of the Working Group have often, in fact, been the most well-attended sessions of the Sub-Commission.

The Working Group was established very much as a result of lobbying within the 'Western Europe and other' (WEO) group, including EC Member States; and it is perhaps appropriate that Western Europe, with its patchwork ethnic culture, should have taken a particular interest in the problem. European experience, of course, concerns the treatment of minorities rather than indigenous peoples. But there is considerable overlap. Indeed, much of the debate at the UN has centred on to what extent you can differentiate between indigenous, minority and tribal groups. Certain Asian countries, in particular, have rejected the concept of 'indigenous' in respect of their own societies, expressing the view that 'we are all indigenous'.

The Working Group is still in the process of considering a set of draft principles for indigenous rights, which, if it is to be adopted and considered at higher levels in the UN system, will undoubtedly provoke much hostile reaction. A central issue in this connection is the extent to which an indigenous people might enjoy the 'right' to call for self-determination, though this is recognised in the UN Charter (Art. 1, line 2) and in the International Covenants (Art. 1) of 1966.

The 'right' to self-determination, however, has never been very clearly defined and it is not clear in what circumstances this might imply self-government. It would seem fair to say that at present there is no great desire among states to focus attention on such problems. The political changes in East and Central Europe have made governments increasingly nervous about addressing 'territorial' issues — though they are being increasingly confronted by such issues. The Gulf crisis has provided one further reminder to Western Europe that much of the border-drawing that forms the basis of today's international system was done frequently very arbitrarily — by the European ex-colonial powers. Sometimes the colonial frontiers may be generally accepted, in the interests of political stability, but sometimes such stability is won at the price of considerable discontent and visible injustice. Often arbitrary determination of frontiers is accompanied by a reluctance to recognise the rights of minorities who find themselves, inadvertently, on the wrong side of boundaries which they themselves had no part in determining. There are many states which reject the very concept of minority recognition, leave alone rights.

Iraq, where the rulers have traditionally been Sunni Moslems over the Shiite majority, is one example of a country which does not accept the concept of a minority. Another example which comes readily to mind is its neighbour Turkey. Members of the Human Rights Subcommittee and Members of the EC-Turkey Joint Parliamentary Committee have had pointed discussions on the status of the Kurdish population.

In this perspective, the European Community, which, for the most part, has managed to come to terms with its minority issues, can be seen as a progressive force. Nevertheless, in the Basque country, in Corsica and in Northern Ireland separatist tendencies remain at the root of extreme inter-communal violence. And we should be very careful when we say that our problems are essentially different from the problems of Aborigines in Australia, the Ahmaddiya Community in Pakistan, the people of the Chittagong Hill Tracts in Bangladesh, or Albanians in Kosovo.

Today, after the Cold War, it is easier to see more clearly, as we look round the world, a pattern of the world's trouble spots and conflicts not being so much ideologically-based, as tribal intercommunal rivalries. Think only of South Africa, the Arab/Israeli conflict, Cyprus, Sri Lanka, Burma, the Horn of Africa, Kashmir, Armenia/Azerbaijan.

We should not forget that, in many instances, it is simply an accident of history that a particular group — the Armenians, for example — have not achieved nationhood. Experts have used different criteria in assessing how many communities could be legitimately seen as 'national' peoples — ranging from 500 to more than 5,000. The UN Commission has referred to 200 million indigenous people throughout the world.

It can be seen, therefore, that such issues are not ones that can be easily approached, but are matters which the world community will be more and more required to face as ethnic tensions increase.

A significant initiative here by the UN Commission has been to authorise a study of national experience in the protection of minorities, in connection with its continuing work on the drafting of a declaration on the rights of persons belonging to national, ethnic, religious and linguistic minorities.

As far as the European Community is concerned, the problems these issues raise were reflected, as mentioned earlier, in the difficulties encountered in Copenhagen at the June 1990 CSCE 'human dimension' conference in reaching a common view on minority issues.

Positive and Negative Human Rights Developments in Third Countries

Although the avowed purpose of this report is to review the human rights situation in the world, as well as to examine Community human rights policy, activities and institutional developments, your rapporteur has included in this explanatory memorandum only a small part of the information about human rights abuses in specific countries made available to him by Parliament's research staff. In view of the contentious nature of this report in earlier years, it is felt that statements (and judgements) about the situation in third countries should figure principally in the motion for resolution, on which Parliament as a whole can take a position, rather than in this 'Part B' which is the responsibility of the rapporteur. It is not always easy to determine what the facts are, since the evidence is often uneven, and coloured by political judgements.

As has been the pattern with previous reports, rather than seeking exhaustively to report on the situation around the world, the resolution has sought to pinpoint where there has been significant progress or improvements with regard to respect for human rights, and where the situation has worsened. Many of the observations in this explanatory memorandum have been made in this perspective, but for the reasons outlined above, mention of specific countries has been kept to a minimum in order not to anticipate the way Parliament may vote in the references to individual countries contained in the resolution.

Your rapporteur would stress here, however, that though much of what has happened in 1989 and 1990 is very encouraging, providing some grounds for optimism, the figures for human rights violations continue to make very stark reading. Some 40 to 50 countries are reliably reported to routinely practice torture, in some cases leading to death. Many thousands of long-term political prisoners or prisoners of conscience languish in jails around the world. The phenomenon of summary executions remains widespread. Political killings and disappearances are a fact of life in many countries, with the re-emergence of 'death squads' in certain countries where this had been thought to be under control, and emerging evidence of the phenomenon in countries where it had previously been brought to light. Secret interrogations, trials and sentencing were common judicial practice in many countries. The lives of indigenous peoples were increasingly under threat. In situations of war and civil conflict, which remains as great a plague as ever, there have been summary executions of prisoners, acts of individual or collective terrorism, torture and execution of hostages, indiscriminate bombings and the use of banned weapons. Such conflicts were the biggest cause of the world's swelling refugee population. Not even children were exempt from these phenomena, with young people in a wide range of countries being unjustly imprisoned, tortured and killed by agents of the state.

Thus, the positive changes in a number of countries should not lead us to the conclusion that the degree of suffering, as a result of human rights abuses, was on a significantly lesser scale.

One consolation, however, is that the picture may seem bleaker because we now know so much more. There are fewer and fewer countries which are closed to the eyes of the world. Human rights activists are able to get information about their situation to the world outside; and inside repressive countries it has become harder to stifle the dissenters. Modern technology is playing a significant role. The telephone, the calculator, the photocopier and the personal computer are proving very much a match for the thought police.

Progress towards Democracy

This report has already touched upon the political developments in East and Central Europe, a subject about which so much has been and is being written (including in a number of European Parliament reports) that your rapporteur will not dwell on this at length. It would seem more useful here to seek to establish to what extent the evolution towards greater pluralism could be described as a 'trend' throughout the world, and the extent to which 'Western' concepts of democracy are being aspired to, or established in, 'non-Western' parts of the globe.

For many in the West, there appear to be few doubts on this score. The final communiqué of the summit of the Group of Seven in Houston, in July 1990, referred in its opening paragraph to a 'renaissance of democracy throughout much of the world'. It also included a political declaration subtitled 'securing democracy', which stated, *inter alia*: 'As we enter the final decade of this century which we intend should be a Decade of Democracy ...'.

If pressed further, however, the seven might have come up with somewhat differing views as to what constitutes democracy. It goes without saying that the 'will of the people' is not merely as expressed through the ballot box. The holding of 'free and fair elections' is not of itself a sufficient guarantee of true democracy. This must be supported by an appropriately pluralistic institutional order. To what extent does the democratic process go on at many levels below that of the nation state, and at regional and local level? To what extent are women, who are commonly the majority, or ethnic or national minorities, active in the process? To what extent do workers participate in decisions involving the production process? To what extent is a society sufficiently pervious to allow the masses to refresh and renew the 'cadres' who in effect govern? One thing is clear — that democracies, however defined, still remain a minority among existing nations. But the changes towards democracy or, at least, greater pluralism, among a very large span of the world's nations, are very significant. We need only look at Eastern Europe where, within the space of four months, six Warsaw Pact countries which had suffered from single-party domination for longer than four decades, suddenly became free to elect governments of their choice. In this brief time, multi-party democracy gained one hundred and sixteen million voters in our own continent.

Looking further back, the past 18 years have witnessed a remarkable European swing toward democracy, restored in Greece and Portugal in 1973 and 1974, and Spain in 1977, thus making Western Europe fully democratic for the first time in its history. Since then, attention has turned particularly to Latin America. More recently, the change to pluralist societies in Eastern and Central Europe has had repercussions in other parts of the globe, Africa for instance, and Asia. As Communist states successively embrace more pluralistic doctrines, Alexis de Tocqueville might yet be proved right in his observation, in 1835, that the principle of democracy 'is universal, it is lasting, it constantly eludes all human interference, and all events as well as all men contribute to its progress'. Although Stalin's inheritance is everywhere in full retreat, the forms of society that will ultimately evolve in Eastern Europe and elsewhere are by no means evident. To return again to Francis Fukuyama, your rapporteur is by no means certain about the inevitability of 'The universalisation of Western liberal democracy as the final form of human government'. It would be comforting to believe that the established democracies in Europe were able and willing to guarantee economic assistance and collaboration on a scale sufficient to ensure the survival of Eastern and Central European pluralism, leave alone its 'finality'.

So far, the optimism of de Tocqueville's definition has not been borne out by history. By the end of the last century, elected governments had been established in much of Western Europe, the United States and some parts of Latin America. During this century there has been a general consolidation of democracy in those regions, though it also lost ground for long periods. The right-wing dictatorships in Europe in the 20's and 30's marked but the most significant phase of regression. It could be said that, after World War I, democracy died in Germany, Italy, Austria, Poland, the Baltic States, Spain, Portugal, Greece, Argentina, Brazil and Japan.

World-wide, after World War II, certain newly-independent nations such as India, Israel and the Philippines all adopted democratic constitutions, as did Turkey and several Latin American countries, and also, from the late 1950's, some of the newly-decolonised nations in Africa. In most cases, however, the experience was short-lived, and most of the newly-liberated colonies and countries in Latin America came under authoritarian or military rule.

But, though pluralism could be said to have lost ground in the 1960's and early 70's, it has been making progress since, with an apparent 'explosion' of the democratic idea in the past few years.

We must, of course, define our terms carefully here. Degrees of pluralism vary greatly from country to country. As stated earlier, the mere holding of elections is not itself a guarantee, despite Joseph Schumpeter's classic definition of a democracy as a political system whose leaders are chosen through regular elections in which candidates freely compete and virtually the entire adult population is eligible to vote. A rather better definition might be: 'a state in which no-one holds power over others without their direct consent, in which all authority is held ultimately accountable to those over whom it is exercised'.

We know, however, from our own experiences that democracy remains highly imperfect. It can contain within itself very authoritarian structures. It can nurture an establishment which is not subject to significant control or easily changed, and it can suffer institutional rigidity — to the extent that the system can, on occasion, be described as one of elective dictatorship.

In many countries democracy is, in effect, a little understood aspiration. One may ask what the students at Tiananmen Square or in Burma (now Myanmar) understood by the concept of democracy. And in advocating it, the European Community and Western nations should be careful to take into account differences of culture, political tradition and economic development. One may or may not agree with the proposition of the Polish political philosopher, Leszek Kolakowski, that the desire for freedom may be a genetic characteristic of the human race. It seems incontrovertible that it has been a continuing and recurrently dominant aspiration in larger parts of the globe throughout all recent history.

Certainly, the determination of voters in Burma to go to the polls in 1988, and in Haiti in December 1990, despite intimidation, and with no recent experience of democratic tradition, was revealing. Indeed, the revolt in Burma which preceded the elections was a rare example of genuine popular uprising, with moral force being opposed to armed force. Another example might be Mongolia, the oldest Socialist country in Asia, which in 1990 became the first such state to witness a multiparty parliamentary election.

Nevertheless, most political scientists agree that to successfully establish democracies certain preconditions are necessary, such as a certain level of economic development, a significant educated class, a tradition of tolerance and respect for the individual, the presence of independent social groups and institutions, a pluralistic economy and, not least, the establishment of conditions in which elites become ready to give up power.

If this is so, then there are many nations of the Third World which seem to stand little chance of soon evolving toward pluralism. Nevertheless, democracy — however it may be understood — does seem to remain a truly international aspiration, and a process in which the world increasingly participates. The referendum in Chile in December 1989 called and lost by a 15-year old dictatorship, was a political process where the rest of the world was present. The election in Nicaragua in February 1990 was almost an 'international election'. (On both of these occasions, European Parliament delegations were on-the-spot observers along with representatives of the rest of the international community). One might also mention that 1989, in Argentina, saw the first transition of power from one popularly-elected president to another since 1922. The subsequent stresses in that country only underline how difficult that process has been.

As we know, however, the hard part comes later. The consolidation of a democracy, which can provide a framework for the respect of human rights, can be a very difficult struggle. In Latin America, though one may say that Cuba and Surinam are the only remaining single party states, the fragility of the democracies throughout the sub-continent is manifest.

Nevertheless, there are significant examples of democracies which have been established and endured in what would not appear to be the most propitious circumstances. India, for instance, has been democratic since independence in 1947, interrupted only by Indira Gandhi's 1975-77 emergency rule. In contrast, neighbouring Pakistan has been characterised, since 1947, by authoritarian civilian governments or military regimes. The experiment with democracy under Benazir Bhutto looks as if it may have been a short-lived experience.

It might be worth recalling that one of Ms Bhutto's most significant international initiatives was in a speech at Harvard University on 8 June 1989, when she called for the creation of an Association of Democratic Nations, the objective of which would be for countries to help one another in fostering and consolidating democracy, especially in countries without long-standing traditions of representative government.

Other bodies or foundations to promote democracy also have sprung up in recent years, and the European Community and its Parliament have supported the establishment of the International Institute for Democracy and the Commission of Democracy through Law, in the framework of the Council of Europe. There are also the longer established Center for Democracy and the National Endowment for Democracy, both in Washington.

There are a number of factors which may render a nation more or less hospitable to democracy. Of course, economic prosperity is one of these. But there is also a variety of cultural influences which can be important in determining whether democratic roots may easily flourish. It may be, for instance, that some religions are more open to democratic forms of organisation than others. Certainly, some religious groupings are more egalitarian than others, and different religions may foster widely divergent attitudes to authority. On the surface, most religions might be thought to have certain difficulties with the concept of pluralism.

How far do such factors influence development? In the Arab world, for instance, the influence of pluralism which we have been detecting elsewhere, has not been very visible. Why? Is it a question of economic resource? Hardly: both the richest and the poorest countries in the region have authoritarian governments. Is the Muslim faith hostile to democracy? Many of us would contest such a conclusion, on both historical and doctrinal grounds. Are there other cultural explanations? Must we examine the reciprocal influences between old empires, out of which the modern patterns of statehood emerged?

To ask these questions is only to reveal the impossibility of providing satisfactory answers in a work of this kind. But we can notice that the spread of independent organisations for the promotion of human rights has been slow in the Arab world, and has encountered many difficulties.

In looking world-wide at developments towards greater pluralism, there is no doubt that the changed position of the Soviet Union on the world stage must be a most significant factor. Moscow is depriving much of the Third World of both a model and a supplier. Africa provides some of the most interesting examples of this. In April 1990, President Mobutu in Zaire announced he would allow certain opposition parties to compete for power and would turn the day-to-day running of the government over to a new Prime Minister. Benin has renounced Marxism-Leninism in favour of private enterprise; and Gabon and the Ivory Coast have moved towards pluralistic systems. Tanzania has also said 'yes', in principle, to pluralism, and in Zambia it has become a matter of public debate which is to be put to the test in a referendum. Newly-independent Namibia joined Botswana, Senegal and Gambia as the only African countries to allow truly contested elections and freedom of speech. Zimbabwe's President has announced an end to the country's 25-year-old state of emergency, renouncing sweeping powers which include the right to detain an individual indefinitely without trial. Significant shifts of this sort must have reinforced a tendency among Western nations to call on African countries not just to engage in economic reform, but to couple this with political reform. There is also, perhaps, a greater willingness to change and look for new ways in view of the manifest bankruptcy of the policies that had been applied in Africa. According to a recent World Bank Report, the gap in *per capita* income between sub-Saharan Africa and the rest of the Third World keeps widening significantly, making the region 'the Third World of the Third World'.

To what extent should the European Community seek to impose its views in such regions? There are examples of how influential Europe can be. The prescription for Benin's 'revolution', for instance, came largely from France, coupled also with significant additional aid. Also in Zambia, as well as social unrest, the need for foreign aid was a significant factor in leading President Kenneth Kaunda to accept, in principle, the notion of pluralism.

Certainly, objectively, Africa would not appear to enjoy the necessary conditions for the establishment of democracy. There is scant democratic tradition, a small proportion of educated voters, and latent ethnic and tribal rivalries. The Ivory Coast, for example, numbers at least 60 different ethnic or tribal minorities. In Zaire there are some 200.

Kenya is perhaps the most interesting example of Western influence. This free-market economy, whilst enjoying traditional Western support, has come to be seen as increasingly repressive, and President Daniel Arap Moi is firmly opposed to multi-party democracy. Recently, there has been much less Western investment, even disinvestment, which may well lead to further social unrest, and demands for change. In the past year, a movement for multi-party democracy has gained strength, and this is something the West could foster by adopting certain policies if it so chooses. President Arap Moi has described democracy as 'foreign ideologies peddled by some unpatriotic peoples with borrowed brains'.

Reverting to an issue mentioned previously, there is little question that easing the debt burden in the Third World can significantly influence for the better the political situation in third countries. There has been an evident trend in Latin America to support populist candidates who promise radical solutions to break the debt squeeze. To put it crudely, unless scarce capital can be put into the local economy instead of being used to repay foreign debt, the prospects for democracy are likely to fade. Very few election campaigns in Latin America do not make debt a major issue. It is no overstatement to say that this problem can lead to social unrest, political adventurism, repression, xenophobia and even killings. It can also increase the levels of hostility to the advanced countries, which are widely perceived as sharing the responsibility for the misadventures of the Third World. UNICEF has warned that if current trends continue, the debt problem alone will cause the deaths of 18 million children a year by the end of the century. There is no question that debt is a major cause in the downward spiral in the standard of living and economic stagnation.

This is a situation which has become very much aggravated during the 1980's. In Latin America, for instance, the decade saw an end of the reasonably low interest rates of the mid 70's. Between 1980 and 1985 the per capita gross domestic products of the region's seven largest economies declined by an average of 8.9%. During the 80's, leaders like Alan Garcia Perez in Peru, Carlos Andrés Pérez in Venezuela, Carlos Menem of Argentina and Fidel Castro put forward and, to some extent, tried to put into effect radical solutions. Economically, South Americans are wont to call the 80's 'the lost decade'. However, it was at the same time a decade of greater political progress. Somoza was toppled in Nicaragua in 1979. Then, Ecuador in 1979, Peru in 1980, Argentina in 1983, Brazil and Uruguay in 1985 witnessed the restoration of democratic institutions and governments. In some instances, it could be said the civilians were given their chance because the military felt they could not handle the economic problems of a complex society, or international pressures. Colombia, in 1990, marked a generational breakthrough in a country long ruled by old men with the election as President of Cesar Gavinia, who is pushing through a plan to call a constitutional assembly to reform Colombia's limited democracy.

But there have been steps backwards. Guatemala, where Vinicio Cerezo Aréval was popularly elected in 1986, has seen a dramatic return to severe human rights violations. Peru is another example. Inflation, unemployment, political violence and general misery all soared during Alan Garcia's five-year term. Garcia, considered to be one of Latin America's most promising young leaders when he took office, was succeeded, in 1990, by the 'outsider' candidate, Alberto Fujimori. Meanwhile, the Maoist Shining Path guerrillas have more and more of the country under siege.

Latin America had, up until the events in Eastern Europe, been the focus of international attention with respect to growing democratisation. It is also an area where Europe has a real role to play. The residual bitterness *vis-à-vis* the United States has meant that, at best, there is a significant triangular relationship involving Europe. It was symbolic that, in June 1990, a delegation from the Chilean Parliament visited Strasbourg to establish closer relations between Chile and the Community, as well as to present the new Chilean democratic reality, following the establishment of the National Congress on 11 March 1990 and the inauguration of President Alwyn.

In Asia, there have also been significant moves towards democracy in many countries. In the Philippines, President Aquino, against the odds, stagnation of economic growth, continuing threats from military rebels on the right and communist insurgents on the left, still presided over the fragile democratic institutions she established, though instituting reform has been more difficult.

Myanmar, known as Burma until late 1989, saw one of the most dramatic popular thrusts to establish democracy. Even at the approach of the 1989 elections, Amnesty International in a report accused Myanmar of operating 19 torture centres, routinely brutalising political opponents by beatings and various forms of torture or ill-treatment. The number of political prisoners was estimated at between 5,000 and 8,000. And yet in the June elections, held under very restrictive conditions, the people made their voice heard. The opposition won by a landslide. Despite severe restrictions on their campaigning, the National League for

Democracy stunned the military government and surprised the world by taking nearly 400 of the 485 legislative seats in an election where there was very little electoral intimidation or vote tampering, and bringing electoral victory — though not power — to Aung San Suu Kyi,[9] daughter of the founder of the modern Burmese state.

Major changes also are underway in Taiwan with presidential elections and other democratic changes to take place to replace a political system that has guaranteed Kuomintang rule for the past four decades.

In Nepal, an increasingly passionate popular movement forced some democratic commitments from King Birendra, who lifted the 29-year-old ban on political parties, and appointed a committee to advise him on constitutional reform.

The events of the past two years should not give grounds for complacency; rather, we should look to making our democracies work better. Many commentators have suggested that, with the apparent ending or diminishing of East-West conflict, East-West tensions will be replaced by North-South ones. The wealthy industrialised nations, with ageing populations, like Western Europe, the United States and Japan may thus be ranged against the have-not nations of the Third World, where, in many instances, half of the population will be under 18. There must also be a concern that, in our own societies, democratic policies have focused more and more on political campaigns and party marketing. An earlier sense of social solidarity and civil obligations has been attenuated. The questions that millions of newly-enfranchised citizens in Eastern Europe are asking themselves about their societies are, perhaps, questions we also should be asking ourselves.

We might also ask ourselves pointed questions with regard to our relations with other countries worldwide — ranging from China to Iraq. To what extent are we advancing our values, and to what extent favouring interests of state? China no longer gives short-term expectations of political reform, which had been encouraged from 1979 to 1989. It is now the most important of the hardline Communist one-party states. Alongside Vietnam, North Korea and Cuba, it is rejecting pluralism on principle. Iraq was not Europe's 'Public Enemy Number One' during the 1980s. At times it seemed as if Syria was. What has made the West so dramatically alter its views?

We are going to have to ask ourselves many such questions in the years to come. What is to be our relation to Central Asia? Upheaval in that region cannot be isolated from the outside world any longer. Will democracy invade from the West? Or Fundamental Islamism from the South? Furthermore, is it not likely that democracy by itself can keep a multinational federation like the Soviet Union together?

Your rapporteur is not sure. Perhaps the movement towards democracy will maintain its impetus. If so, this can only be welcomed by Parliament. One must remain conscious, however, that democracy is not an easy attainment, and once achieved it must be nurtured and protected.

Conflict Resolution

The end of the arms race between the USSR and the USA produced a détente in which, for a time, a number of peaceful settlements became possible in long-standing trouble spots. Wherever in any zone there was direct friction between the two superpowers, it became possible, by agreement, to encourage United Nations intervention in pursuit of solutions. Beyond doubt, this enhanced the authority of the United Nations as a mediator. It could assume responsibility for the reaching of agreements, even if such agreements depended on the goodwill of the greatest states. Hitherto, the relations between thse two had been so strained as to preclude almost any possibility of joint action. In such circumstances, the Security Council could not intrude in a very large number of disputes, even in cases in which its help might have been materially effective.

With cooperation among the permanent members of the Security Council, various actions became possible. Thus, there appeared to be some progress towards conflict resolution. The revolutionary upheaval in Eastern Europe passed off peacefully in every country except Romania. Secretary-General Perez de Cuellar had seemed to be on the verge of achieving significant breakthroughs in Western Sahara, Cyprus, Afghanistan, and, indeed, in the Iran/Iraq war itself, where the carnage had dwarfed that in all other conflicts during the time in which it ran.

In Southern Africa there seemed a prospect for an end to the 14-year Angola war, and in neighbouring Mozambique, also, positive progress was registered. Some months on, some of these breakthroughs seem less evident. The Community must continue to do what it can. It did, for instance, identify early what would be needed on the humanitarian plane to establish 'normal' life in Afghanistan — though the continuance of the conflict, despite the 'peace settlement', has prevented this policy from being put into place. In similar fashion, it has begun to identify the needs of a pacified Indo-China, and should look to playing a significant role in that region. In other conflict areas, such as Central America and the Horn of Africa, the Community continues to seek to target its aid with a strong sense of the political context.

In Southern Africa, 'the two steps forward, one step backward' situation appears manifest. The liberation of Nelson Mandela (who addressed the European Parliament on 13 June 1990) and movements by President de Klerk have undoubtedly been positive. Nevertheless, from a human rights perspective, it must be stated that while there would appear to have been political progress, and significant rapprochement between the ANC and the government, violent conflict seems as much as ever a feature of South African life.

Elsewhere in Africa, some 20 wars were recorded during the period under review, with Liberia providing an example of perhaps the most insensate carnage. The wars in the Horn of Africa rage unabated, despite the call in June 1990 by Presidents Bush and Gorbachev for a UN-sponsored conference to settle the civil wars in Ethiopia, the Sudan and Somalia. In the Middle East, there is the *Intifada*, the strife in Lebanon and the Iraqi conflict triggered by the invasion of Kuwait.

Looking around the world, although progress towards peaceful settlements has undoubtedly been made in a number of long-standing trouble spots, it must unfortunately also be recorded that new conflicts have emerged — for instance, in the Asian republics of the Soviet Union.

For a time the UN has enjoyed enhanced authority, underpinned by the new entente between the United States and the Soviet Union. Before that, relations between the United States and the USSR were so strained as to preclude any joint action. The Security Council virtually ignored the war between Iran and Iraq for seven years.

Another example worth watching closely is the little reported cooperation beginning to develop between the US and the USSR on Central America. Will it enhance the right to constitutional development in freedom, or will it simply establish a condominium for oppression?

It is too early to assess the results of cooperation between the superpowers in the matter of the Gulf conflict. Early expectations spread the hope of 'a new international order'. After the outbreak of war, more and more people came to fear the intensification of a very old order, involving the conflict of the North and the South. If such a conflict is to develop, the prospects for human rights will become dim indeed. If it can be avoided, then perhaps it is possible that the United Nations might begin to pull its full weight for the first time.

One matter that should not be overlooked is the need for enhanced protection for victims of war. In January 1990, the Red

Cross and the Red Crescent launched a world campaign for the Protection of Victims of War. The object was to sensitise public opinion and governments to the fate of war victims and provide more support for international humanitarian law. This matter was touched on in a report adopted by the Political Affairs Committee, under derogated procedure from plenary.[10] (The Subcommittee is also to draw up a report on the protection of journalists in conflict situations.)

Your rapporteur would urge that we look again at devising international codes for the protection of other organisations which do not have the international special status of the Red Cross.

One thinks here of the work by the Europe-based medical organisations who have come to play such a significant role, such as *Médecins du Monde* or *Médicins sans Frontières*, and *Aide Médicale Internationale*.

Human Rights of Children

It goes without saying that war produces the most gross violations of human rights — particular insofar as it affects that most fundamental of rights, the right to life.

We are bound to be concerned about the extent to which children are being enlisted as combatants — for example, in Afghanistan, Angola, Central America, Ethiopia, the Gulf, Iran and Mozambique. Child enlistment was a matter we already identified in the previous report. Unfortunately, it would appear to have progressed negatively, to the extent that it is almost accepted as a fact and an inevitable consequence of conflict situations.

Considerable public attention was focused on this problem when 1989 was declared by the UN General Assembly to be the International Year of the Child. This was reinforced by the adoption (by concensus on 20 November 1989) of the UN Convention on the Rights of the Child. Parliament, at its July 1990 session, urged the European Community Member States to ratify the Convention and to draw up a European Charter to protect children.

It should be noted that one of the more controversial points of the UN Convention is that it does not ban military recruitment under 18. It simply says, 'States parties shall take all feasible measures to ensure that persons who have not attained the age of 15 years do not take a direct part in hostilities'.

The United Nations Human Rights Centre has estimated that world-wide there are 200,000 children under the age of 15 bearing arms.

Many of these are 'conscripted' into rebel/guerrilla groups — the *mujehadeen* in Afghanistan, where boys as young as nine are in the field; by the Karen rebels in Burma; by the FMLN in El Salvador, which also is reported to have enlisted young girls for combat; or by the Renamo rebels in Mozambique, where press-ganged or kidnapped children are not just trained to fight, but also forced to kill and maim civilians.

However, governments also have connived in this — hence the decision not to amend the above-mentioned paragraph from the Convention and raising the minimum age for recruitment from 15 to 18. In those parts of the world where war has become endemic, and where a large part of the population is 'under age', the skills of a trained adult are a precious resource, and untrained children are used without scruple in military operations. The Iranians used even pre-teenagers for front-line combat in the war with Iraq. The Ethiopian and Salvadorean armies also have conscripted boys under 18. One could recall also the *Khmers Rouges* in power recruiting children, often the orphaned victims of B52 bombardments, to kill civilians and even send their surviving relatives to their deaths; or the 'pre-teenagers' who terrorised the people of Uganda as part of Idi Amin's army.

In singling out this issue, your rapporteur is aware that in historical terms it is difficult to say that our own times are 'worse' than earlier ages. In earlier centuries, under-age soldiers have been commonplace, and children have been commonly 'used' in conflict situations. Little or no distinction is made for children in inter-communal violence. Children, as we can see from our own times, whether throwing rocks in the *Intifada* or in Northern Ireland, are often only too willing to volunteer to earn the respect of their peers and their elders by fighting. Their motives may often be material: if we accept that 100 million people in Africa wake up hungry each day, three-quarters of them children, we realise that there can be an attraction in being enlisted to obtain 'generous' army rations.

It is hard to see, barring a dramatic diminution of conflict in the world, that this tendency will diminish. The projected models of population growth make it clear that many governments will succumb to the temptation to tap the reserves of their enormous under-age populations in what they deem to be crisis circumstances, requiring military action.

The tragedy is that there is latent aggression in adolescents which can be channelled. We need only look at the teenage gang warfare in urban big city America, and certain European cities, not to mention the almost tribal hooliganism of some UK football supporters. It is difficult to generalise sensibly about this extremely complex sociological and psychological issue. But is it not self-evident that this latent aggression in young people can be tapped and encouraged by their elders? Whose admiration are children seeking to earn, but their elders'? Indeed, in fighting, are some children aspiring to 'adulthood'.

In a world where the threshold of violence has arguably increased, we should be aware of the damage being done to future generations. This generation is probably pushing that threshold even higher. Look only at what in the United States have come to be called 'mushroom killings' — the deaths of children in street violence or in domestic conflicts, particularly in big urban centres such as New York or Los Angeles. Children exposed to brutality at an early age, either as perpetrators or victims, will be that much more likely to inflict that brutality on their societies when they become adults.

At the very least, the international community must do everything possible to prevent adults from 'encouraging' regard for violence through force of arms. Education should not expose impressionable minds to 'war games'.

It would be too long a task here to detail the extent to which civilian women and children have been victims of human rights abuses by armies and security forces. There has been widespread disregard of the Geneva Conventions concerning civilians. We may recall the 'Cayara Massacre' in Peru in 1988 where schoolboys were among the 29 villagers tortured, then shot, hacked or clubbed to death by masked or hooded soldiers. Or we may cite the 'Halabja' massacre of March 1988 in which 5,000 Kurdish villagers endured an agonising death by chemical weapons, at the hands of Iraqi forces. During the 1990 session of the UN Commission on Human Rights, the Special Rapporteur on Torture, Mr Peter Kooijmans, said he was particularly alarmed at communications he had received concerning the torture of children. In Iraq, for instance, the Special Rapporteur has listed reports of routine torture even against the children of political opponents. Lest it be thought that these examples relfect current preoccupations in the Gulf crisis, we hasten to add that Amnesty International has published worrying reports about the similar use of torture in Syria, Turkey and Iran, amongst other nations in the same region.

However, states must be made to account for all human rights abuses of under-age persons. We know, for instance, that youngsters were also among the 'disappeared' in certain countries of Latin America such as Argentina.[11] Palestinian children have been victims of human rights violations almost every day since the beginning of the *Intifada.* According to United Nations figures, more than half the casualties recorded in the Gaza Strip during the first year of the *Intifada* were under 15 years old. Amnesty International has stated that children were shot dead by Israeli forces. Others have been severely beaten, imprisoned after unfair trials, and administratively detained without charge or trial. Many were involved in incidents in which stones or other missiles were thrown; but others appear not to have been involved in any violent activities before they were shot or apprehended. In South Africa, as has been recorded in previous annual reports, very high numbers of children are in detention, many of whom have suffered torture and ill-treatment. An estimated 9,800 were detained under state of emergency regulations between June 1986 and June 1989. (Children in prison in South Africa were the subject of a resolution adopted during the 1990 session of the UN Human Rights Commission.) Amnesty has also reported many instances of criminal abuse of young persons by armed forces in such countries as Iraq, Iran, Peru, Sri Lanka, Guatemala and Brazil.

Guatemala and Brazil are examples of societies for which there are clear parallels in our own, where children are marginalised. It is estimated that about seven million children in Brazil live apart from their parents on the fringes of society, often in conflict with the authorities. Frequently, they are the victims of police violence and ill-treatment in custody. Colombia is another example, where thousands of children scratch out an existence as beggars and thieves, outside any state care network. We should note that in Colombia there has developed the remarkable foundation, 'Los Ninos de Los Andes', established by the crusade of one man, Jaime Taramillo, and his wife Patricia.

What can we do to ensure that the UN Convention is not merely a document, but an instrument to change government policies? The Convention requires 20 ratifications to bring it into effect, which should take place some time this year. The European Community should give all possible support to the Committee on the Rights of the Child, made up of experts, set up to monitor compliance with the Convention, which, for most purposes, defines a child as a person under the age of 18. For instance, countries which ratify it will undertake not to execute or imprison for life people whose offences were committed when they were children under the age of 18.

It is noteworthy in this connection that the US Supreme Court, by a narrow 5-4 majority, ruled on 26 June 1989 that the execution of juvenile offenders was possible under the US Constitution. In

August 1989, no fewer than 27 prisoners in the USA were on death row for crimes committed when they were less than 18 years old. The most recent Amnesty International report documents the execution of juvenile offenders in Iran, Iraq, Bangladesh, Pakistan, USA and, it was believed, Nigeria.

Nevertheless, we must recognise that the new convention repeats guarantees which already exist under the International Covenant on Civil and Political Rights, which recognises the vulnerability of the young and children's need for special protection. Governments often contend that human rights abuse of young persons is an unfortunate consequence of their involvement with street crime. It must be clearly stated, however, that crime control is no excuse for the violation of the basic human rights of children, including the right to life.

These problems are, of course, far from unfamiliar in our own societies, and there has been particular concern during the period under review at the exploitation of children. Child abuse and child pornography have received considerable public and media attention in Western Europe and the United States.

Internationally, during 1990, this was the focus of the UN's Working Group on Contemporary Forms of Slavery. A resolution by the UN Commission in March 1990 called on all UN member states to consider how appropriate action might be taken for the protection of children and migrant women against exploitation by prostitution and other practices verging on slavery, including the possibility of establishing national bodies to achieve these objectives.

Under a draft decision on the sale of children, the Commission decided to appoint, for a period of one year, a Special Rapporteur to consider matters relating to the sale of children, child prostitution and child pornography, including the problem of the adoption of children for commercial purposes. The rapporteur's conclusions were to be presented to the 1991 session of the Commission.

His conclusions may provide some global perspective on the true scale and nature of a problem which has, until now, been highlighted mainly by individual alarming reports concerning, for instance, child labour and debt bondage. Defense of Children International, for instance, has reported that children were being kidnapped in Pakistan and sold into forced labour camps. Mention should be made here, however, of the very careful monitoring activity which has been performed over the years by the Anti-Slavery Society, that doyen of human rights NGOs.

Even when childrens' rights are not deliberately abused, this is an almost inevitable by-product of famine, war and refugee situations. In view of the demographic tendencies in some of the most ravished regions of our planet, there must be great fears that, unless we single out the young for special protection, their situation will deteriorate further.

Parliament has in the past[12] laid stress on the importance of human rights education, but as yet there is scant budgetary provision for this, either at national or Community level. In addition to singling this field out for attention, your rapporteur would wish — as the Political Affairs Committee sought in amendments tabled to the 1990 European Community budget — to provide more financial assistance to child-oriented projects by the European Community, particularly those providing concrete on-the-ground assistance.

It is only by focusing our attention on children that we can have some hope that the future will be brighter than the past, that this generation does not pass on to the next the burden of its fears, prejudices and hatreds. We can, if the international community cares enough, prevent a situation in which it is normal that children should be enlisted as front-line soldiers.

Regional Human Rights Systems

Parliament has always, in the past, attached considerable importance to the promotion and support of regional human rights systems. This has seemed natural in view of the European perception that it is our own regional system which is the principal framework on which we must rely for the protection of human rights in Europe. It has also seemed appropriate wherever one accepts that one cannot neglect cultural relativity when defending human rights, and that some allowance must be made for regional 'context'.

One might here mention, in passing, one negative effect of regionalisation. It has become apparent that at the UN the trend is increasingly for countries to coalesce into regional blocs. This has meant, in effect, that no denunciation of a country can take place without the agreement of countries of that region. Asian countries, at the 1990 session of the UN Commission, blocked censure of Iraq, Iran, Burma and China. On Cambodia, ASEAN countries would not modify their position.

When we consider the evolution of regional systems and mechanisms, we find that it is currently in Europe that the greatest movement is taking place — or, at least, is under discussion. There has been much talk of a very general level, in the light of events in

Eastern Europe, of what Vaclav Havel has called a 'politics of ethics', of 'civic culture'.

At the institutional level, your rapporteur and the previous annual report have both alluded to the problems of institutional overlap — principally between the European Convention, the case law of the European Community Court of Justice, and national constitutional and legal provisions.

As well as these considerations, we must now take into account the evolution of human rights mechanisms in the wider Europe. These were addressed at the November 1990 CSCE summit, in connection with Basket III. NATO, in the London Declaration of July 1990, wanted CSCE to have a secretariat to service regular high-level consultations, a mechanism to monitor elections, a centre for the prevention of conflict, and a parliamentary Assembly of Europe. Already the issues are being actively discussed. In June 1990, in Istanbul, the Justice Ministers of the 23 Council of Europe member states met, significantly, with the presence, as observers, of justice ministers from East Germany, Hungary, Poland, Czechoslovakia, Canada, and a Vatican representative.

The '23' have declared themselves in favour of a framework convention for the protection of the human person against abuses of the biomedical sciences. They took the view that the universality of these rights implied that the states should protect them at national level, 'but also in the broadest possible international context'. The drafting of this Convention (which will be open to countries which do not belong to the Council of Europe) has already begun.

With regard to the role of the Council of Europe in the rapprochement with Eastern European countries, the Ministers declared that the gradual adhesion of these countries to the legal heritage of the 'Europe of the 23' will favour their adhesion to the Organisation as full members. The Council was invited to establish an Action and Assistance Fund (to which voluntary contributions will be made) in order to promote this rapprochement. The Ministers also invited the Council of Europe to: i) draw up an inventory of the priority needs of those countries in the legal area and in the area of human rights, ii) to establish an exchange programme between specialists for the elaboration of legislative and constitutional drafts, as well as the organisation of the judicial branch. Lastly, they recommended that the Council of Europe should add a declaration which would reaffirm the fundamental character of the primacy of law and pluralist democracy within the current context of pan-European integration.

The primacy of human rights in building the new Europe was underscored at the November 1990 summit which drew up the

'Charter of Paris for a New Europe'. The opening section of the Charter was headed: 'Human Rights and Democracy — The Rule of Law'.

Elsewhere in the world institutional development of pan-regional human rights systems has been less dramatic. There has, however, been a remarkable upsurge in the number of human rights NGOs and local grass roots groups. The phenomenon has been clearest in Eastern Europe. The previous report drew attention to this phenomenon, often linked to political opposition, in Latin America and Asia. We now see it, too, in Africa. Human rights NGOs and monitors are now becoming an organised force, their work publicised and encouraged by groups like Africa Watch. A major lacuna is the Arab world, though we should not neglect the valiant work of the Arab Lawyers Union, which speaks on behalf of lawyers in 16 Arab countries, and who (rather pertinently in view of the developments in Iraq in 1990) have, for 3 years, been alerting international bodies that Iraq must not be neglected, and have also been stating that human rights protection in the entire Arab region was worsening.

It should also be mentioned that there now exists a draft charter of human and peoples' rights in the Arab world; and also an Arab League Draft Convention on Human Rights, and the proposed establishment of an Arab Commission on Human Rights.

If put into effect, this would certainly represent progress. But we should not indulge illusions as to the extent that such documents might have teeth. A relevant example for comparison might be the African Charter of Human Rights and Peoples adopted by the Organisation of African Unity in 1981. This came into effect in 1985 and is still not over-vigorous. But there is progress. There have been more ratifications of the Charter in the past two years, and, since June 1990, the African Commission — the monitoring body established under the African charter — has for the first time a permanent headquarters in Banjul, Gambia.

Last year's report referred to the case brought by the Inter-American Court of Human Rights and the Organisation of American States in considering a case brought by the Human Rights Commission of the Organisation of American States against a member state, Honduras, concerning the disappearance, torture and assassination of four nationals of Honduras and Costa Rica. The Court found the Honduran government responsible for the 'disappearance' of Manfredo Velasquez Rodriguez and ordered Honduras to pay damages to his family. Subsequently, it has reached a similar decision with regard to Saul Godinez Cruz, and also ordered the government to pay compensation to his family. These instances represented the first time that an international judicial body had ever dealt with disappearances or death squad killings.

We should also mention here the trend to establish national human rights commissions — as in Morocco and Mexico. An open mind is necessary to weigh this development, although openmindedness involves a necessary degree of scepticism, particularly in so far as these official bodies may frequently attempt to act as a counterweight to local NGOs.

African, Caribbean and Pacific Countries

The major development in the period under review has been the signing of the Lomé IV Convention. Significantly, the references to human rights in the Convention were strengthened. We must now seek to establish, as soon as possible, what is the exact significance of the new changes.

Your rapporteur will not dwell on human rights within the ACP framework. This question is covered in the opinion of the Committee on Development and Cooperation. Considerable progress, however, would appear to have been made in developing the dialogue on human rights with our ACP partners.

This, and provisions in the previous Lomé III Treaty, has set an important precedent for other international agreements. The most significant was the agreement between the Community and the countries party to the General Treaty of Central American Economic Integration. There is also the 1990 trade and cooperation agreement with Argentina, which includes a clause, at Argentina's request, concerning human rights.

How far, in view of the references in Lomé IV, should we be seeking to exploit these provisions? We were prepared to raise human rights forcefully with Eastern Europe, and Parliament must press for human rights clauses in the 'second generation' agreements with Eastern Europe now being negotiated. Why not then with Africa, where the European Community has had an institutional partnership for many years?

A major impediment to more effective action in this field may well be our own doubts about how far linkage is appropriate between development assistance and acceptable standards of human rights.

Some progress in our own discussion now seems essential in view of the thinking at the World Bank and IMF that aid should become increasingly conditional with regard to Africa. In June 1990, for instance, the British Foreign Secretary, Douglas Hurd, in a major speech on Africa, said: 'Political pluralism, respect for the rule of law, human rights and market principles' would bring donor support coordinated by the World Bank and the IMF, and even possibly private investment'. This raises the whole issue of 'conditionality', which up to now has been resisted by the European Community: it also poses the question of whether development aid should be allocated *a priori*, or subject to continuous checks on human rights performance.

Within this context, the proposal to institute a human rights monitoring system in the newly-created European Bank for Reconstruction and Development (EBRD) has to be looked at with some care. On the one hand, respect for human rights, including the right to food, health and education, is a serious matter and an important objective of international policy. The aim of the founders of the Bank was to foster 'multi-party democracy, the rule of law, respect for human rights and market-oriented economies'.

A well-noticed paper from the New York Lawyers' Committee for Human Rights seeks to establish that all these aims run together, and, when they do so, guarantee in any country credit-worthiness and its probable effective use of loans. No evidence is given for these assertions, except for the general claim that curtailment of human rights in Eastern Europe 'must have' impaired productivity and economic initiative, and some personal observations of the General Council to the World Bank which are quoted. Indeed, it would be hard to prove, or to disprove, such generalisations. To do so, we should need measures of human rights observance, of market orientation and of effective use of finance, which we do not have. There are enough examples, however, of human rights abuse, in countries like Turkey and South Korea, which have successful market-oriented economies, or in countries like Romania and South Africa, which have successfully repaid loans, to raise doubts of the correlations.

The most serious questions have to be raised about the nature of market orientation. This is sometimes referred to as 'open-market-oriented economics', sometimes as 'respect for market economics'. The degree of market orientation does not appear to be correlated, at least in developing countries having similar debt problems to those of Eastern Europe, either with economic success or the effective use of loans. The United Nations Economic Commission for Africa and UNCTAD have both strongly questioned the basis for all the claims of the World Bank that African countries, which strongly reformed their economies towards market criteria, fared better in the 1980s than those that did not. The managing director of the IMF himself, Mr Michel Camdessus, stated in 1989 that 'too often in recent years it is the poorest segments of the population that have carried the heaviest burden of economic adjustment'.

We must ask whether the lawyers may not have got it the wrong way round: is it not economic deprivation and disorder that lead governments to the abuse of human rights?

The problem becomes even tougher when we try to take note of the good advice given in the 1990 World Development Report of the World Bank, which recommends that a government's record on poverty alleviation should also be considered during negotiations about international loans.

How can all these conflicting conditionalities apply? In the words of the Brundtland Report (*Our Common Future*, Oxford, 1987):

> 'To require relatively poor countries to simultaneously curb their living standards, accept growing poverty and export growing amounts of scarce resources to maintain creditworthiness reflects priorities few democratically elected governments are likely to be able to sustain for long.' (p.75)

Now, to this difficult set of economic imperatives we are to add the directly contradicting social imperative, to curb poverty: and to compound the question, we prescribe full pluralism, democratic choice, and human rights.

The only thing we do not prescribe is the phalanx of saintly angels who know how to deliver such a combination of goods to regions whose actual experience is of choking deprivation, misery, ignorance, and economic and political manipulation, often by cynical outsiders.

The United Nations Human Rights System

In the past, this report has sought to reflect trends in the UN human rights system, which though it falls short of its early aspirations, remains the foremost international standard-setting body and one which the international community, not least the Twelve, must seek to make work more effectively.

During the period considered by this report, despite criticisms levelled at the UN, it must be said that the organisation has enjoyed considerably enhanced prestige. Mention already has been made of the role of UN mediation in El Salvador, Cyprus, Western Sahara, Afghanistan, the Iran-Iraq war, Namibia and Cambodia. A durable peace has not always been the outcome, but the UN has played its part. It was appropriate for the Nobel Peace Prize to be given to the 'blue hats', above all because of their development of mediatory approaches. It is worth noting that the European Community, for instance in Cyprus and the Iran-Iraq war, looked to a UN framework as the most appropriate negotiating framework within which a dispute could be settled. Also, during the large number of elections which have taken place around the world, the presence of UN monitors to supervise has been important.

To look more specifically, however, at the UN's human rights activity — centred on the Commission and its Spring sessions of 1989 and 1990, and the Sub-Commission on Prevention of Discrimination and Protection of Minorities — one must conclude that there have been very few new institutional developments in the style of operation of the organisation.

Nevertheless, important progress was made with regard to 'standard-setting': On 15 December 1989 the UN General Assembly adopted the Second Optional Protocol to the International Covenant on Civil and Political Rights aiming at the Abolition of the Death Penalty. This is the first universal treaty providing for legal abolition of the death penalty and recognising it as a human rights issue, with possible derogations resulting from a state of war. Any state party to the Covenant can adhere, and it is to be hoped the European Community will take heed. In addition, the Economic and Social Council adopted a resolution, endorsed by the General Assembly also on 15 December, calling for certain conditions with regard to application of the death penalty — mandatory appeal or review, maximum age limit, exemption for the mentally retarded.

In a related ECOSOC measure, also endorsed by the General Assembly on 15 December 1989, principles were agreed on the Effective Prevention and Investigation of Extra Legal, Arbitrary and Summary Executions, attempting to curb the phenomenon of extrajudicial executions.

Most international attention focused on the Convention adopted by the General Assembly on 20 November on the Rights of the Child — a matter your rapporteur has singled out as especially relevant, particularly in view of the growth of the world's under-age population, in the changing demography of the globe.

With regard to all three of the above measures, the contribution of the Twelve was significant. Your rapporteur would stress again the importance of the Twelve working and voting together at UN human rights bodies — still not always the case (as at the 1989 session of the Commission in resolutions concerning Cuba).

While recognising the UN's pre-eminent standard-setting role, previous European Parliament reports have been critical of the reticence of UN bodies. They have been too reluctant to take up some clearly documented patterns of abuse in individual countries. Positive initiatives have been stale-mated by diplomatic horse-trading within diplomatic alliances. It was thus pleasing to see, in view of the Political Affairs Committee's public hearing in February 1989 on Romania and numerous European Parliament resolutions (before the revolution in that country), that the Commission on Human Rights decided to appoint a Special Rapporteur on the human rights situation in Romania. Also positive was the attempt, initiated in 1989 after Tiananmen, to consider the human rights situation in China and request the UN Secretariat to report to the 1990 session of the Commission on Human Rights. But in 1990, the Commission, after intense lobbying, refused to vote the resolutions tabled by Western countries on China, and on Iraq. Despite evidence made available, the situation in these countries was not pursued. This put the credibility of the Commission in question.

Regrettably, as mentioned earlier, there seems to be a tendency for regional blocs to emerge to protect their number (for instance, Latin American countries, although they broke ranks on Cuba in 1990, allowing the United States to get 'its' resolution). This is especially true of Africa which in 1991 prevented consideration of the situation in Somalia. This phenomenon may be exacerbated as Northern countries look South (and no longer East) to 'condemn'. The continuing pressure over Cuba exerted by the US delegation, headed by Armando Valladares (to which reference was made in the previous report), is an example of the kind of diplomatic action which can further prompt regional blocs to close ranks.

Another regrettable tendency at the UN is an apparent pressure to exclude participation of NGOs, who, far more than nation states, speak out clearly on human rights. Your rapporteur was most encouraged to see the strong statement made in defence of the role of NGOs at the 1989 session by French Prime Minister Rocard. The European Community should resist all tendencies to minimise or restrict the role of NGOs in connection with the changes now being developed to 'reform' the UN system — with some restructuring, procedural changes and a reduction of the number of seats reserved for Northern Countries, or increasing the number of Members of Commission. European countries have come forward with other concrete propositions — rationalisation of agendas, strengthening of thematic rapporteurs, creation of a mechanism between sessions, boosting resources of UN Centre, better discipline of participants.

It is also worth noting that the Commission is seeking to enhance cooperation between the United Nations and regional and national institutions for the promotion of respect for human rights. Both the European Community and the European Parliament should seek to foster cooperation of this kind. To this end it would seem appropriate that the European Parliament be represented at the World Conference on Human Rights decided by the UN General

Assembly Resolution of 15 December 1989. Your rapporteur, in this connection, would like to pick up the idea already advanced that the European Parliament should apply for observer status (like, for instance, the Council of Europe or the OAU) to certain UN human rights organisations. Previous rapporteurs have called, in particular, for EC observer status at UNHCR. Parliament's President has called for closer EP association with the FAO, and the Chairman of Parliament's delegation for relations with the UN, in December 1990, called for EP/EC association with the work of a range of UN agencies.

Here we note that the welcome trend — suggested by the European Parliament and started in 1989 — in which the Twelve speak as one at the UN on human rights, has continued in 1990. At the 46th session of Commission on Human Rights, at ECOSCO, and at the Third Committee of the 44th General Assembly there were common positions. Statements of the Twelve, in 1989, included the message on the occasion of the International Day of the UN for the Elimination of Racial Discrimination (21 March), and the statement by the Presidency on behalf of the Twelve concerning the Implementation of the Programme of Action for the Second Decade to combat Racism and Racial Discrimination (12 May).

It is encouraging to see that in the statements by Foreign Ministers Ordonez and Collins the emphasis and affirmations directly followed the lines advocated by the European Parliament in annual reports. The European Community even voted together in 1990 on all the resolutions on the Occupied Arab Territories.

It is no accident that the 1990 session saw what could have been described as more North-South tension. But it should also be noted that the Central and Eastern European countries, while now playing a constructive role, have also begun to outline their own particular priorities and perceptions with regard to human rights and how they think the UN system should evolve.

It is significant that the new Romanian government accepted that the mandate of the Special Rapporteur on Romania should be extended (not usually the case when a country emerges from dictatorship). It is also interesting to note how East European countries are not always acting as a group: Yugoslavia, for instance, was isolated, not being proposed by the East Europe group to be part of the Working Group on the Effectiveness of the Commission, even though it was chairman of the non-aligned group. This may have been because of Yugoslavia's perceived over-reaction in Kosovo within the Working Group on Minorities of which it is Chairman.

The extent of dual standards within the UN system was unfortunately shown up over Iraq and China. Iraq, under international pressure on its human rights record for three years, managed to find a procedural way out. It is instructive to contrast this fact with the new continual flood of criticism of Iraq's systematic breaches of human rights. China escaped censure by sustained lobbying in a close vote (the size of the Chinese delegation at the Commission was more than 40 diplomats). The extent of lobbying of a country to defend itself, to garner support from other nations in its region and use procedural devices, does perhaps testify to the value of the UN system and the seriousness with which it is taken.

Overall, there were perhaps no great innovative changes; but they may come, and be for the worse: the working group on improving the functioning of the Commission may not in the end be deemed to have come up with what we might consider improvements. The Twelve must ensure this is not the case.

It was also encouraging that the mandates of five 'thematic' rapporteurs (a development the European Parliament has welcomed in the past) was prolonged for a further two years. It should be noted here that the non-aligned group sought to reduce their effectiveness by requiring that all material submitted to the UN by individuals should be referred directly to Confidential Procedures, thus escaping the attention of the thematic rapporteurs. The work of Mr Wako (summary executions) and Mr Kooijmans (torture) should be singled out as especially valuable. Their capacity to visit individual countries is becoming of far more significance than the routine complaints procedure to the Commission. What is regrettable is that their reports on visits to specific countries go uncommented at the Commission. Your rapporteur is strongly of the view that the 'theme procedures' should be strengthened and that their capacity for 'effective action' should be enhanced and independence of rapporteurs be maintained.

Overall, though, it was too early in the period under review to report major changes; and it is up to the Twelve to continue together to seek to bring about more reforms and transparency, and resist the 'tactical bloc' approach which more than anything else stymies and falsifies the work of the Commission. If anything, the UN Sub-Commission is more politicised than ever. In 1990, there was even a secret vote on 'flagrant violations of human rights throughout the world'.

The European Parliament, which always has stressed the importance of human rights education, welcomed moves at the UN Commission, in 1990, to boost its information/education activities on human rights, creating materials and programmes, in national and local languages, with specific target audiences in mind. There also was continued commitment to the provision of advisory services and technical assistance, not least within the World Public Information Campaign for Human Rights.

It should be noted that at its 46th session, in 1990, the Commission took up one of the themes of the '89 session, and the UN called on all Member States to support such campaigns and, for instance, to include in their education curricula materials relevant to a comprehensive 'understanding of human rights issues' and encouraged all those responsible for training in law and its enforcement, the armed forces, medicine, diplomacy, and other relevant fields, to include appropriate human rights components in their programmes.

The European Community should heed this request. Although there have been previous attempts to increase funds in the European Community budget for human rights education, including reception of human rights *stagiaires*, little progress has been made. The European Parliament should, therefore, seek to enhance budgetary provisions of this kind. It should be noted that there exists a UN Voluntary Fund for Advisory Services and Technical Assistance in the field of human rights, which is directed partly towards providing expert and technical assistance to governments with a view to creating and developing the necessary infrastructures to meet international human rights standards.

Finally, your rapporteur would stress the key role of the Sub-Commission and its working groups, despite criticisms that it is devoting too much of its time to issues already being considered by the Commission and other UN organs. It should be noted, however, that Sub-Commission experts all too frequently are government officials, not 'independent experts', as originally intended. The Sub-Commission also remains a more reliable indicator, for instance, indicating its belief that certain countries are responsible for a consistent pattern of gross violations of human rights, even though the Commission subsequently decides not to pursue consideration of these countries.

The Role of the European Parliament and Community Policy

Consideration or observation of the UN system, which is essentially a set of delicate inter-state negotiations about human rights, leads one to look at the European Parliament's and the European Community's possibilities for action in a rather positive light. It reminds one that Parliamentarians are not representatives of states, but of their electors. They, therefore, have a capacity to speak more independently and less diplomatically. As the world's only elected international Parliament, it is appropriate that the European Parliament should address human rights problems in countries throughout the world. Not only is this legitimate, it is expected. The European Parliament's human rights 'post-bag' is large and diverse, and Parliament constantly receives appeals to act, intervene or take a position not just from individuals but also from numerous NGOs and human rights groups.

It has been stated that Parliament has given too high a profile to its human rights activity, that it is out of all proportion that at every part-session resolutions on perhaps five or six different human rights issues should be voted; or that of the written and oral questions put to the Council and the President-in-Office of the Twelve, some two-thirds should concern human rights. Such public declarations, however, are largely a response to the concerns of the electorate, and to the internationalisation of the human rights movement, which is essentially sustained by the concerns of individual citizens. Public consciousness about human rights abuses is probably higher than at any time in human history, to the extent that human rights has been described as a 'new gospel'. As citizens of the world, people no longer feel that events such as Tiananmen Square or Timisoara are a matter outside their concern.

There also appears to be a public perception of the European Parliament as an international actor in the sphere of human rights, that groups of Members or bodies of Parliament are willing to actively campaign to correct a perceived injustice.

Nonetheless, we have reason to be modest about the results of our work. The European Parliament is certainly a magnet for human rights approaches, and is in turn itself extremely good at spawning human rights initiatives. What it lacks, however, is adequate machinery to follow through its initiatives with the requisite determination and persistence. This may be a failing, or a characteristic of parliaments in general, and not just of the European Parliament. Similar criticisms have been made of the US Congress.

The big difference with Congress, however, is that human rights there are an aspect of congressional legislative activity concerning agreements with third countries. (The Foreign Assistance Act of 1961 provides for this, and these provisions led Congress to call for the State Department's annual report to Congress on human rights.) Also, Congress has managed to establish as of the mid 1970s within the executive, a bureaucracy centred on the Department of State concerned with the implementation of United States human rights policy. Your rapporteur would not wish to over-emphasize the role which the State Department's Bureau of Human Rights and Humanitarian Affairs plays in policy formulation. What is significant, however, is that it exists, has significant resources, and has sought to give greater emphasis to human rights concerns in US foreign policy formulation.[13]

The European Parliament has had considerably less success in prompting the Commission and European Political Cooperation to establish appropriate structures; and with the exception of one or two countries, European nations have not established sections or departments for human rights or made human rights reporting a specific obligation of embassy officials. Certain diplomats do have a coordinating role, but this usually is concerned most specifically with the preparation of positions for UN and CSCE human rights bodies.

As mentioned earlier, the genesis of Parliament's 'annual report' was a proposal, at one of the first meetings of Parliament's Working Group on Human Rights, that EPC submit to Parliament each year for a major debate an annual report, in the way that the Department of State reports to Congress each year.

The idea was actively pursued by the Working Group and the Political Affairs Committee, but there was a clear unwillingness of EPC to travel down the road that Parliament was advocating. One senior official told a working group chairman that, even if there were agreement to establish a structure, it would not be possible for the Twelve to formulate common views on human rights situations on a global basis, because of distinct differences in perception and foreign policy thrust in the foreign ministries of the Twelve. (It might be remarked, in passing, that even the US State Department's report is said to give rise each year to extensive debate and dispute with regard to how the situation in particular countries should be presented.)

Subsequently, in 1985, EPC was to submit the first of its annual memoranda on the human rights activities of the Twelve (1989 and 1990 memoranda), and later still it was to follow the suggestion of the European Parliament that a Working Group on Human Rights be established within EPC, at meetings of which Commission officials also participate. Human rights matters are also a specific competence of one of the officials of the EPC Secretariat established by the Single European Act of 1986.

These structures, however, remain skeletal; and, despite the importance which European Political Cooperation has accorded to human rights, they remain, in your rapporteur's view, inadequate to fully pursue human rights initiatives. This problem was addressed very clearly in remarks by the head of the EPC Secretariat,

Ambassador Iannuzzi, to the Political Affairs Committee in September 1989. He stated:

> 'The main feature of the requests put by the individual MEPs in questions and by Parliament as a whole in resolutions, is their sheer volume, which makes them very difficult to follow up, and also their sometimes unrealistic nature. Over 70% of all the questions concern specific human rights cases, mostly in countries or situations in which the Community has no real means of intervention or where, if it did intervene, it would be interfering in a manner which would seriously compromise the very causes it is called on to defend.'

Such counsels of restraint have not led Parliament to desist in its efforts to keep human rights very high on its agenda. Regrettably, however, it has not even had the will within its own Secretariat to create a significant bureaucratic structure to underpin and prepare its human rights commitments and initiatives. There has been some progress in this sector with the establishment of a small 'Human Rights Unit' in 1984, the staff of which was boosted in 1990 and 1991. However, this remains insufficient, and does not serve to lend credibility to the European Parliament's human rights activity. Your rapporteur would look to more progress being made in this regard, and has strongly supported moves to strengthen the 'Human Rights Unit' and integrate it to a greater degree into the European Parliament's Committee Secretariat (DG II).

Looking ahead, this would appear to be more necessary than ever. The previous annual report and some observations earlier in this explanatory statement have identified a need for the European and national institutions concerned with human rights to cooperate much more closely on an inter-institutional basis. This kind of cooperation would appear to be even more necessary, if we look ahead to the establishment of a 'concentric circles' Europe, with what may very well have the European Community at its core. If, as seems likely, the Council of Europe and a restructured CSCE become key institutions in the 'second circle', the European Parliament and the European Community must be able to relate to them in a meaningful way.

There was a strong sense of such developments in the CSCE 'human dimension' conference in Copenhagen in June 1990, which was visited briefly by a small delegation from the Human Rights Subcommittee. It was the perception of Members that very probably CSCE structures based on Basket III will evolve, although also a concern that this should be in concert with, and not overlapping with, the Council of Europe. These concerns seemed to be recognised by participants at the November 1990 'Helsinki II' summit in Paris. It cannot be ignored that the Council of Europe, or more particularly the European Convention on Human Rights and its Human Rights Court have been the pre-eminent standard-setting normative regional human rights body in Europe.

Returning to the Community, it is important that we do not lag behind in the establishment of structures, whether *vis-à-vis* the Council of Europe, CSCE, the United States or the Soviet Union. With regard to the latter, for instance, an extremely useful dialogue has been initiated by the Human Rights Subcommittee with its counterpart Subcommittee of the Soviet Union. This has led to the resolution of a certain number of individual human rights cases. But, if the European Parliament is to make concrete suggestions that will seriously be considered by the Soviet authorities, using the norms already established in Western Europe as a model, it must have the resources to carry forward such a dialogue. In addition to exchanges with the Soviet Subcommittee's Chairman, Mr Burlatsky, in Brussels, an invitation has been received for a delegation from the Subcommittee to visit Moscow. Such a visit can be very useful but only if it is properly supported so that carefully prepared positions can be put forward.

As far as human rights work inside the Community is concerned, the agenda is certainly there, as is hoped will be recognised from some of the issues addressed earlier.

Indeed, it could be very considerably amplified. Suffice to look at the agenda and documentation drawn up for the Strasbourg Conference on human rights and the European Community — 'Towards 1992 and Beyond', 20-21.11.1989. It is particularly disheartening to see that the most impressive body of work and scholarship produced for the conference has not generated any significant response or further initiative on the part of the European Community institutions. There may be a feeling that much of the programme is over-ambitious, thinking too far ahead. Your rapporteur's view is that the issues identified may arise rather sooner than anticipated, in which case a degree of preparation to affront them would appear necessary.

They may indeed arise, and your rapporteur would hope that this is the case, as a result of the proposals at the inter-governmental conference in the course of this year (for instance, in connection with the Spanish proposal on 'European citizenship'). With regard to European Political Cooperation, it should be recalled that the provisions of Article 30 of the Single Act, concerning EPC, are due to be revised in 1993. If, as seems likely, they are further developed, additional human rights provisions and structures will have to be a factor of the revised Treaty.

One consequence seems certain to be that EPC becomes integrated much more fully into the work of the European Community. In this connection the Single Act can be seen as an interim phase. There is no need to dwell on the logic of this development. Suffice to say that it now seems to have been clearly recognised that even if the Twelve can seek to formulate policy in distinct areas on an intergovernmental basis, their means of action and their power to meaningfully articulate that policy lies principally through the Community.

In this connection, your rapporteur would point to the network of commercial and cooperation agreements, of which the Community is the nexus, and which makes the Community a major actor — in economic and trade terms — on the international stage. The relationship engendered by these contractual arrangements gives the Community a considerable capacity for influence. Although probably a majority of MEPs would stand by the notion that *pacta sunt servanda*, they do at least provide a framework whereby — if it so chooses — the Community or one of its institutions can express its human rights concerns.[14] More significantly still, it has now become feasible to provide a legal justification for advancing human rights concerns within the text of an agreement. This began with references to human rights and democracy in the Lomé Treaty and has been followed in other international agreements referred to earlier.

The inclusion of such references on a systematic basis could be much further developed — for instance in the 'second generation' of agreements with the countries of Eastern Europe, where negotiations have already begun. In this connection, one should not forget the role of the Parliament in giving its assent to agreements negotiated under Article 237 and 238 of the Rome Treaty, as amended by the European Single Act. Even on agreements not subject to assent, the European Community can seek to ensure that human rights considerations are taken into account. The Parliament, last year, on human rights grounds called[15] for the PHARE programme not to be applied to Romania; and human rights considerations will play an important role in determining European Community policy on Indochina.

There are difficult problems involved in judging how far to use the restriction, or threat of restriction, of economic intercourse as a weapon to punish infractions of human rights. If threats work, of course, there will be few who will argue against their use. But supposing they do not? Then they are either shown to be idle utterances, easily to be ignored, or a rupture of exchange must ensue. What is the result of such a rupture? It is difficult to generalise about this.

When the issue of the Jackson Amendment was debated in the United States a dozen years ago, the Soviet historian, Roy Medvedev, argued against the restriction of trade between the USA and the USSR, on the grounds that the extension of all such linkages constituted an encouragement to human interaction, and therefore afforded scope for the development and protection of human rights. Your rapporteur was most interested to hear the same argument from Professor Fang Lizhi, widely known throughout the world as the 'Chinese Sakharov', when he was able to leave the hospitality of the American Embassy in Beijing for exile in Britain and the USA. Professor Fang also stressed that it would be difficult to influence Chinese behaviour by cutting back on trade exchanges, since the vast dimensions of the country gave its leaders wide freedom of manoeuvre, in substituting one product for another, and practising autarchic responses. Autarchy is the last thing that Chinese democrats wish to promote, since it will set back their desire to come closer to the wider world.

This is not to say that certain economic sanctions may not be entirely appropriate. Firstly, where prison populations are producing for export, would-be recipients of such exports may well wish to choose similar products from elsewhere. Of course, prison reformers might instead seek to take the opportunity trade offers to insist on a code of conduct, and rights of inspection, in penal institutions producing objects for exchange in the market place. Does not this depend upon the reasons for which people are locked away? These are matters which afford a range of options. Such choices may be made in accordance with over-arching principles, or they may be deployed tactically, to achieve concessions and exact reforms. A boycott may be brought in to signify disapproval, or held in prospect as a possible deterrent to executions or other excesses in the treatment of 'crime', real or imaginary. The logistics of a human rights campaign of this kind remain to be thoroughly explored.

However we decide these questions, it is clear that Parliament cannot allow itself to measure with different yardsticks. We have no way of applying to China, whatever our commercial interests, different standards from those we have in the past found relevant in our dealings with Israel, or South Africa, or the USSR. Should we be less concerned for the rights of national and ethnic minorities in China than we have been elsewhere? Why do Mongolians differ from Estonians or Eritreans, for instance? If we are not absolutely convinced that the rights of five million people in Hong Kong will be respected, what is the morality of coercing them into absorption into a State whose record, since June 1989, has aroused so much anguish? It will be argued that, under treaty, the territories of Hong Kong must revert to China in 1997. But must the people revert, whether they like it or not? Freedom of movement has been given, by the British Government, to a section of the important business and professional classes. Wealthy Hong Kong citizens have been able to buy citizenship by investing in Canada. But what of that mass of the population upon which Hong Kong's phenomenal economic successes have been built? The right of exit would avail them of far better prospects than might intermittent interruptions of commerce. It might also offer a strong incentive to the Government of the People's Republic of China to develop benevolent policies towards those who choose to remain.

At the same time, however, as arguing for a consistency of morality in our contacts with third countries, your rapporteur recognises that with regard to human rights, the Community and the Parliament are constrained to be selective. The European Community's policy is not to sanction itself out of commercial existence[16]. Equally, the Community only has the resources and political will to focus on a limited number of targets. To have any effect we must be selective. It is the only way we can be effective. Nevertheless it is easier for the European Community as a community to be active than it often is for an individual Member State in bilateral contacts, where we so often see blind eyes turned, or incontrovertibly untrue statements made about a third country, when it seems politically or commercially expedient.

The need to be selective is frequently why the European Community so often seems to find itself embroiled in a human rights dispute with nations with which we are closely linked, such as Israel and Turkey, rather than with nations whose human rights records, such as Burma and North Korea, are undoubtedly worse. It is of our friends and neighbours that we expect the highest standards. We judge Israel and Turkey by our own standards, not by those of some of their Arab neighbours. To ignore the human rights situation in Turkey — a country which is a candidate member of the European Community — would be worse than irresponsible. Your rapporteur thus much welcomes the dialogue on human rights that has now been initiated between the Subcommittee and the Turkish members of the Turkey-EC Joint Parliament Committee. It is to be hoped that this dialogue may eventually lead to a direct link between the Subcommittee and the newly-established human rights committee of the Grand National Assembly. Whether or not this will have any effect in a country which theoretically applies international norms, but which in practice flagrantly abuses them, is open to question. Yet Turkey should be left in no doubt about the seriousness of our concerns and that these concerns will guide the spirit of our relations. They should also be left in no doubt that we will be equally assiduous at identifying and following up instances of abuse within the European Community, for instance, with regard to the rights of Turkish workers within the European Community; that as well as examining the situation of the Greek minority in Albania, we also will take an impartial view of the situation of the Turkish minority in Komotini. The latter may perhaps be easier said than done in view of the very particular nature of the relationship between Greece and Turkey, but the Community must be rigorous with itself to the extent of divisiveness if Turkey is to see the earnestness of our purpose.

The European Community's relationship on human rights also needs to be seen as not merely one of sanction, or carrot-and-stick. It must be seen also as the initiator of positive programmes and measures aimed at enhancing the respect for human rights. This is one of the reasons why the Human Rights Subcommittee has begun to pay particular attention to the funding of human rights-related activities in the Community budget. As well as in development programmes, funds exist in a number of budget lines for projects with a human rights bias. The number of budget lines is rather larger if you also take in political/human rights issues which have become an object of European Community policy — such as extension of the PHARE programme, the Programme of Positive Measures in South Africa, and trade policy with the Occupied Arab Territories.

There is concern, however, that the allocation and targeting of funding and identification of priorities has in the past been somewhat *ad hoc*. For this reason, the Political Affairs Committee in 1990, albeit at a very late stage, decided to nominate for the first time a draftsman of an opinion to the Budgets Committee on human rights spending. It should be said here that Parliament has been particularly remiss in not seeking to articulate sufficiently clearly a budgetary strategy and criteria, and to signal clearly to the Commission when these priorities change. The Parliament cannot blame the Commission for what may result as a consequence of its own incoherence. Thus, your rapporteur would wish to see the Human Rights Subcommittee at least attempt, in future years, to orchestrate the budgetary strategy that the European Parliament wants to see put into effect.

At the end of the day, much of the European Parliament's or the European Community's action might be dismissed as merely rhetorical, much of its spending devoted to projects which simply help small voices to shout louder. But the power of verbal persuasion should not be under-estimated. Countries around the world today want to be numbered among the 'good'. The European Community is perceived in the world as a significant moral force, as befits a 'civilian' power, and the European Parliament, in particular, can afford to be very concrete and even, when necessary, 'undiplomatic' in the targets it identifies.

The European Parliament does not represent 'national' interests — happily, since there is frequently a conflict of interest between human rights and the interests of states. And, curiously, its pronouncements appear often to be treated with greater respect by third countries than by Community Member States. Within the Community institutional framework it is clearly the Parliament which has sought more than any other institution, perhaps appropriately, to make the European Community active in the human rights field, not simply paying lip service to human rights. Your rapporteur trusts that this impetus will continue, and that the word 'active' will be an accurate description. Despite the foregoing remarks about the power of verbal sanctions, your rapporteur is convinced that the European Community and the Parliament need to be actors on human rights. No country should be left in any doubt as to the sincerity of our commitment to human rights, or of our determination to use all the means at our disposal to advance them.

References

1. Resolution A3-166/90 on the Intergovernmental Conference in the context of Parliament's strategy for European Union (OJC 231 of 11.7.1990, p.97).
2. OJ C36 of 16.1.1986, p.142.
3. OJ C176 of 11.6.1986, p.63.
4. A3-195/90 — The Findings of the Committee of Inquiry into Racism and Xenophobia.
5. B3-1721/90 and B3-1722/90; OJ C284 of 10.10.1990, p.57.
6. PE 143.354/A and PE 143.354/B/rev.
7. cf. Opinion of Political Affairs Committee to Budgets Committee on 1991 draft budget (PE 144.022/fin.)
8. Sub-Saharan Africa: From Crisis to Sustainable Growth, 1989.
9. In 1990, Aung San Suu Kyi was awarded the European Parliament's 'Sakharov Prize' for Freedom of Thought.
10. Doc.A2-43/89 on international humanitarian law and support for the work of the International Committee of the Red Cross (ICRC); OJ C120 of 14.4.1989, p.342.
11. Prevention of the disappearance of children in Argentina, UN doc.E/CN.4/Sub 2 1988 (19(1988).
12. cf. Resolution of Parliament on human rights teaching of 18.10.1982.
13. Edwin S. Monuard, 'The Bureaucracy and Implementation of US Human Rights Policy', *Human Rights Quarterly*, May 1989.
14. cf.Parliament's decision on 9.3.1988 not to give its assent to the conclusion of three protocols between the European Community and Israel (Bull.EC3-1988).
15. Doc.A3-172/90 on political developments in Central and Eastern Europe including the Soviet Union, and the European Community's role (rapporteur: Mr Penders); OJ C231 of 13.7.1990, p.203.
16. cf.Doc.1-83/82 on the significance of economic sanctions, particularly trade embargoes and boycotts, and their consequences for the EEC's relations with third countries, adopted on 11 October 1982 (rapporteur: Mr Seeler); OJ C292 of 8.11.1982, p.13.

PART II

RESOLUTION
on human rights in the world
for the years 1989 and 1990
and Community human rights
policy

The European Parliament,

— Having regard to the motions for resolution by:

(a) Mr Staes on human rights in Guatemala (B3-0003/90),

(b) Mr Arbeloa Muru and Mr Ramirez Heredia on a world-wide amnesty for prisoners of conscience (B3-0062/90),

(c) Mr Glinne on child prostitution (B3-0066/90),

(d) Mr David on the plight of children in the third world (B3-03/90),

(e) Mr Arbeloa Muru on behalf of the Socialist Group on secret executions in Iraq (B3-0497/90),

(f) Mr Newens and others on human rights abuses in Iran (B3-655/90),

(g) Mr Newens and others on assassination attempts against Iranian refugees (B3-1101/90),

(h) Mrs Fontaine on involvement of children in armed conflicts (B3-1479/90),

(i) Mr Arbeloa Muru on measures against torture, violent deaths and disappearances (B3-0033/91),

— Having regard to its resolution on human rights in the world and Community policy on human rights of 17 May 1983,

— Having regard to its resolution on human rights in the world and Community policy on human rights of 22 May 1984,

— Having regard to its resolution on human rights in the world and Community policy on human rights of 22 October 1985,

— Having regard to its resolution on human rights in the world and Community policy on human rights of 12 March 1987,

— Having regard to its resolution on human rights in the world and Community policy on human rights of 18 January 1989,

— Having regard to the report of the Political Affairs Committee and the opinions of the Committee on Development and Cooperation and of the Committee on Youth, Culture, Education, the Media and Sport (Doc.),

A. whereas the first directly-elected European Parliament

undertook to draw up an annual report on human rights in the world and Community human rights policy,

B. whereas a commitment to democratic principles of government and to the protection of human rights and fundamental freedoms under the rule of law is a prerequisite for membership of the European Community,

C. whereas the Community reaffirmed this commitment in the joint inter-institutional Declaration of 5 April 1977, the Declaration on Human Rights adopted by the Foreign Ministers of the Twelve on 21 July 1986 and the preamble of the Single European Act which provides that the Member States and institutions of the EEC are determined to work together to promote democracy on the basis of the fundamental rights recognized in the constitutions and laws of the Member States, the European Convention for the Protection of Human Rights and Fundamental Freedoms and the European Social Charter,

D. whereas, in the period under review, there were references to human rights in the conclusions of the Dublin European Council (June 1990) on human rights and good governance in Africa and of the Rome European Council (December 1990) on the promotion of democracy and human rights in external relations, and in the conclusions of the Council meeting of 19 December 1990 on a restructured Mediterranean policy, containing a Declaration on observance of human rights and the fostering of democratic values,

E. whereas the European Community's commitment to human rights is deemed also to extend to the protection of human rights, *outside* the Community, and the Community's highest bodies have stated that expressions of concern about human rights violations in third countries cannot be considered unjustified interference in the domestic affairs of a third country, and whereas the countries of the European Community, both individually and collectively, have an obligation to seek the enforcement of international human rights law,

F. whereas human rights are universal, not dependent on particular systems of law or government, and governments have a duty to promote them beyond as well as inside their own frontiers,

G. whereas there has been a significant evolution in the international community's perception of its obligation to intervene, by various means, wherever there are grave violations of human rights, reflected most recently in UN Security Council Resolution 688 of 5 April 1991,

H. whereas Community action to further human rights in third countries is inspired by the Community's own legal system, based on the Treaties, the case law of the Court of Justice, Community legislation, the provisions of the European Convention on Human Rights and Fundamental Freedoms, and Member States' constitutions and laws,

I. whereas, if human rights abuses occur in the countries of the European Community, then there normally exist instruments of redress under due process of law (including Community law which now incorporates certain conventional human rights such as freedom of association and freedom of expression), and where such instruments prove inadequate, there are available, in principle, mechanisms which can rectify abuse,

J. whereas despite the competence assumed by the Community in human rights matters, the Community is not endowed in the Treaties with a specific legal mandate in this sphere, and has not adhered to the European Convention on Human Rights, despite calls by Parliament that it should do so,

K. whereas in the forthcoming review of the provisions of European Political Co-operation, and in the new provisions that may result from the Inter-governmental Conference on Political Union, there should be explicit reference to the Community's obligation to promote and protect human rights,

L. whereas regional systems of human rights protection in different parts of the world are becoming increasingly important, and the significance of the 'human dimension' must also emerge as a fundamental aspect of the institutional architecture of the new wider Europe,

M. whereas in Parliament's annual reports particular emphasis is given to three fundamental rights — the right to life, the right to respect for the physical and moral integrity of the person, and the right to a fair trial by an independent court — while at the same time recognising that all human rights, whether political and civil, or economic, social and cultural, are indivisible and intertwined,

N. whereas neither lack of social and economic development nor any persuasion or ideology may serve as a justification for the denial of civil and political rights, nor persuasions and ideologies as justification for the denial of social rights or the right to development, and the European Community must be cautious about holding itself up as a model and in pursuing human rights issues with third countries should always take account of cultural relativity and 'context',

O. whereas there are currently severe threats to human rights within the European Community, not least as a result of the resurgence of intolerance and racism which led to the adoption on 11 June 1986 of the 'Evrigenis' Declaration against racism and xenophobia and a committee of inquiry by Parliament in 1990 drew up a report which called for further concrete measures to be taken,

P. whereas democratic life within the Community is still threatened by terrorism which, during the period under consideration, has been responsible for murders and other criminal acts in various Member States, particularly in Spain, Greece, the Federal Republic of Germany, France and the United Kingdom, sometimes with the support of political forces which are protected by democratic legality,

Q. whereas human rights issues within the European Community such as right of asylum and treatment of refugees, are among the major political issues before the Community, many aspects of which are not covered by the Geneva Conventions of 1951 and whereas in the light of the completion of the internal market in 1992 the EC must seek solutions at Community level which supplement national and international measures,

R. whereas
— there has been considerable worldwide growth in the recognition of human rights;
— a Community based on democracy and the rule of law has worldwide responsibilities because of these principles which it should also incorporate in its foreign policy;
— the European Parliament, as intermediary for human rights concerns from the whole world, must be open to these concerns, to examine them for accuracy to the best of its ability and then to support them through its resolutions,

S. whereas Community citizens rightly demand full respect for human rights on the part of all the Member States and want respect for human rights on the part of third countries to be a fundamental parameter for Community relations with such countries,

T. whereas pluralism and democracy help to protect human rights and increasing numbers of people are insisting on their human rights and becoming aware of their individual rights,

U. whereas human rights flourish best in a situation of democratic stability and it is the duty of Community bodies, and in particular its Parliament, to encourage the evolution of constitutional freedom, democracy and political pluralism,

V. whereas in many more, though not yet all countries, governments have become increasingly sensitive to outside opinion and to representations about their human rights records,

W. whereas it is recognised that action in favour of human rights is a legitimate international activity which cannot be construed as improper interference in the internal affairs of third countries,

X. whereas while international pressure may not always work, it is a proven fact that even governments which violate human rights are sensitive to it and it is moreover a political prisoner's only protection and many former detainees have attested that words can have power and documents be persuasive,

Y. whereas, however, the European Community, no less than other members of the international community, has been 'selective' in its approach and its human rights policies have on occasion been determined by strategic and geopolitical and commercial considerations,

Z. whereas in recent years human rights have been given greater emphasis in the foreign policy of the Community and its Member States and whereas, therefore, clear guidelines should be developed,

AA. whereas
— in a world which is moving closer together, peace can be threatened when human rights violations increase in places where order breaks down and violence and desolation dominate,
— whereas it is not possible for the Community to create stable conditions without a strict observance of human rights,

1.   Reaffirms the undertakings, statements of principle and policy proposals made in its previous human rights reports;

2.   Believes that the period under review (1989 and 1990) gave rise to hope that the international community might make significant advances towards achieving greater respect for human rights, not least as a result of the ending of the 'cold war' and the prospects of an enhanced and more effective role for the United Nations;

3.   Regrets, however, that these hopes and aspirations, inspired by great changes in a number of individual countries, most notably in Central and Eastern Europe, do not permit the conclusion that worldwide the degree of suffering as a result of human rights abuses is on a significantly lesser scale;

4.   Deplores that in addition to war and civil conflict, with the gross abuses that result from them, the majority of governments around the world practise or connive in various forms of human rights abuse and that in a significant number of countries, including those closely associated with the European Community, internationally recognised human rights are flagrantly and systematically abused by means of torture or other violations of the right to life and human dignity;

5.   Notes that the basic principles of international legislation dealing with the safeguarding of human rights are most commonly violated in situations of armed conflict, including, *inter alia*, by summary executions of prisoners, acts of individual or collective terrorism, torture and execution of hostages and captives, indiscriminate bombings, and use of banned weapons;

6.   Believes, in this connection, that gross violations of the Geneva Conventions are more frequent than ever, and notes that internationally reputed humanitarian organisations such as the International Committee of the Red Cross consider that the 1980s saw an escalation of violence around the world, particularly in internal conflicts not clearly covered by international humanitarian law;

7.   Recalls with sadness that during the last 45 years some 105 armed conflicts have taken place, almost all of them in the third world, and that in recent years civil war and inter-ethnic conflict in particular have become more widespread, and that during the 1980s there was a sharp rise in the number of conflicts — international,

internal or mixed — with many of these now of prolonged duration, and that more than 80% of the victims of contemporary conflicts are civilians, the overwhelming majority of them women and children;

8.   Notes further that 13 wars are still continuing in Africa, with the longest lasting conflict in Eritrea, having continued for almost 30 years, and the conflict in Mozambique also of protracted duration;

9.   Is deeply concerned that the use of mustard gas by Iraq against Iran and possibly also the use of cyanide gas and nerve agents, has contravened an internationally recognized rule and notes that as many as 20 countries are now believed to possess chemical weapons or the capability to use them in violation of the 1925 Geneva Protocol;

10. Regrets that the wave of liberalisation which swept across the world during the period under review has had no significant effect on many countries; that with significant exceptions such as the freeing of the world's best-known political prisoner, Nelson Mandela, thousands of long-term political prisoners still remain incarcerated in various countries, and in some cases have been in detention for more than two decades, as in Cuba, Indonesia, Malawi, Syria and Morocco; that between 40 and 60 countries in the world are reliably reported to routinely practise torture, including in some EC neighbouring countries around the Mediterranean basin such as Turkey; that 'emergency legislation' is still unjustifiably used to hold prisoners of conscience without charge or trial, as in Syria where state of emergency legislation has been in force since 1963;

11. Affirms that such phenomena must be squarely blamed on individual governments and their unwillingness to respect the international pacts to which they have acceded, and put into effect preventive safeguards and remedial measures;

NEGATIVE DEVELOPMENTS

12. Draws attention, below, as has been the pattern with previous annual reports, to the consequences of armed and political conflicts, mismanagement and famines which can lead to serious violations of human rights:

I. Refugees and displaced persons

(a) The continuing growth of the world's population of refugees now estimated at 15 million, with a further 20 million displaced persons, with the greatest numbers in South East Asia, Afghanistan, Pakistan, the Horn of Africa, Southern Africa, and Central America, and new problems emerging in such countries as Somalia and Liberia where the 1990 civil war in that country, with its population of 3 million, led to 500,000 displaced persons in the country and 500,000 refugees in neighbouring countries,

(b) The emergence of new refugee problems on a considerable scale in the Middle East, particularly as a result of the Gulf war, and affecting particularly the Shi'ite and Kurdish populations of Iraq; and in Eastern and Central Europe which, for instance, led in 1990 to an estimated net inflow of about 1 million people into the Federal Republic of Germany and, according to Commission estimates, the prospect that some four to eight million persons might seek to leave Central and Eastern Europe, including the USSR in the coming years,

II. Children

(a) The increased marginalisation and vulnerablility to gross human rights abuses of children, as highlighted at the 1990 World Summit for Children, with 15 million infants and children dying each year, according to UN estimates,

(b) The existence of more than 100 million 'child slaves' in the world, with the greatest numbers of labour-exploited children in the Indian sub-continent, though there is also exploitation of under-age labour in certain European countries as in Portugal, Italy and Greece,

(c) Violence against 'street children', as in Brazil and Guatemala in 1990 which saw an epidemic of child murders with street children being gunned down by vigilante groups in many cases made up of off-duty police,

(d) The suffering of the 'street urchins' of Bogota and other Colombian cities who live and die on the streets and are often forcibly recruited as thugs and murderers by gangs of drug-traffickers,

(e) In countries all over the world, the unjust imprisonment, torture, 'disappearances' and murder of children by agents of the state, one significant example being Iraq where hundreds of children have been mistreated, and many of them have disappeared or been tortured,

(f) Failure to protect childrens' rights in other countries such as Guatemala, Peru, Sri Lanka, Turkey, the Occupied Territories and South Africa, where an estimated 9,000 children were detained under state of emergency regulations between June 1986 and June 1989,

(g) The enormous increase in child prostitution, found particularly in countries where per capita income is significantly below the world average, although it is also found, admittedly only sporadically, in Member States,

III. Torture

(a) The persistence of deaths reported after torture in such countries as Turkey, El Salvador, Burkina Faso, Sudan, South Africa, Indonesia, Iraq, China, India, Myanmar (Burma) and Kuwait, with certain countries where the phenomenon of torture had not been previously observed to a significant degree also being reliably identified as in Equatorial Guinea and Kenya where in 1990 there was torture and ill-treatment of hundreds of prisoners of conscience,

(b) The increased involvement of doctors in torture as a result of its practice by increasingly scientific methods, leading to a global campaign within the medical profession to ban such doctors from practising, which led in South America alone (most notably in Chile) to nearly 20 doctors (in 1990) being found guilty of complicity in torture by the ethical commissions of their own professional bodies,

IV. Trade union rights

(a) The violation of trade union rights and liberties in many countries, as was indicated by the General Assembly of the International Labour Conference of June 1991,

(b) The proclamation of laws and/or orders to restrict trade union activities and oppress trade union leaders and activists, leading to disappearances, torture and extra-judicial executions of such trade unionists, solely on account of their union activities,

V. Death squads/extrajudicial executions and 'disappearances'

(a) The resurgence of such extrajudicial killings often arising in situations of international and internal armed conflict, violence between armed groups (guerrillas, drug dealers, police and the military), the reemergence of death squads which appeared to have come under control in certain countries,

(b) The spread of this phenomenon to areas where it had not previously been reliably documented, such as in parts of Asia (for instance, Sri Lanka, India, the Philippines and Myanmar (Burma)); and in Africa, where, for instance, the work of death squads in South Africa is now coming to light; or Mali where there was government-sponsored killing of members of the ethnic Tuareg group, and 55 prisoners were extrajudicially executed by the security forces in August 1990; or Niger, during the same period, where more than 100 Tuaregs were reportedly killed; or in Somalia where in July 1989 46 political prisoners were executed extrajudicially; or in Mauritania where in April 1989 and November/December 1990 extrajudicial executions by the security forces took place; or in Chad, where more than 300 prisoners were executed by the Presidential Guard in December 1990 or starved to death in custody; and in the Middle East, most notably the killing of scores of unarmed Kuwaitis by Iraqi occupying forces in 1990,

(c) The increased number of death threats against individuals in many countries, according to United Nations Special Rapporteur, Amos Wako, who in 1990 wrote to forty-five governments requesting explanations about summary executions about which he had received information,

(d) The continuing practice of 'disappearances' as in Peru, Colombia, Guatemala, El Salvador, the Philippines, Sri Lanka and in China, where dozens of persons arrested in June 1989 remain unaccounted for; and the continuing absence of new information or investigation of long-term 'disappearance' cases, as in Ethiopia, Syria, Morocco, Western Sahara, Guinea, Chad and Cyprus, with many of these cases dating back some ten or fifteen years,

(e) The continuing failure to account for those persons who disappeared following the Turkish invasion of Cyprus,

(f) The coming to light of new information about disappearances in countries where the phenomenon has essentially been eradicated, as in Argentina and Uruguay, and in Chile, with the Chilean Commission on Human Rights reporting that it has documented 2,200 political executions and 900 disappearances under the Pinochet dictatorship; and the tendency to grant immunity from prosecution to alleged violators of human rights, as has been the case in certain Latin American countries with members of the former military establishment,

VI. Death penalty and extrajudicial executions

(a) The carrying out of extrajudicial executions in a number of countries without due process of law or after grossly unfair trials in a number of countries, as in Iraq, Kuwait, Nigeria, Sudan and Iran, which in the period under review saw the end of a three-year period where 5,000 people were reportedly executed without access to a lawyer, no right to call witnesses in their defence, and no right of appeal and, in Iran, in 1989 alone more than 1,000 prisoners were killed in mass secret executions both for 'political' crimes and 'common' crimes, including many in public, including stoning to death for adultery, drug offences, prostitution and living on immoral earnings,

(b) The continuing application of the death sentence in many countries, in some cases on a considerable scale, as in Iran and also in Iraq, where in 1989 hundreds of executions took place on the basis of sentences imposed by special courts without any right of appeal; in China where there was an increase in the already high number of executions after the crackdown on the pro-democracy movement; and in the Soviet Union where the authorities have now begun to disclose annual figures for death sentences and executions which numbered 190 in 1990,

(c) The execution of long-stay political prisoners, as in Indonesia where four such executions were carried out in 1990, with other prisoners still under sentence of death after twenty years in jail,

(d) Rulings in the United States to maintain the death penalty for juvenile offenders, with the Supreme Court in June 1989 stating that execution of juvenile offenders and the mentally retarded is permissible under the US constitution, and the House of Representatives considering in October 1990 an expansion of the list of federal crimes that can carry the death penalty and a limit of appeals by state prisoners who face execution,

(e) The maintenance of the death penalty in Turkey, the only Council of Europe member state to have carried out judicial executions in the 1980s, although the number of offences for which the death penalty can be applied has been reduced, and the death penalty has not been carried out for more than six years, and in 1991, subsequent to the period under review, the Turkish parliament commuted all of the approximately 290 death sentences,

(f) The trend towards abolishing the death penalty which cannot be considered a favourable trend since the death penalty is still found in the legislations of 134 out of 178 countries and is still applied *de facto* in 92 countries. Even if the death penalty continued to be abolished at the same rate as in 1990 (7 countries completely abolished it: Namibia, Czechoslovakia, Ireland, Andorra, Sao Tome e Principe, Mozambique and Hungary, and Nepal abolished it only for ordinary offences) we would have to wait until the year 2000 and beyond to see a world without the death penalty. This is without taking into account the attempts being made to reintroduce it in some countries, such as Brazil in June 1991, in El Salvador and in some Far Eastern countries for drug-linked crimes, and unfortunately the issue of reintroducing it is sometimes also raised in Community legislative bodies,

VII. Indigenous peoples

(a) The increased threat to the lives and livelihood of indigenous peoples as they attempt to defend their land from incursions by ranchers and by mining and timber companies, as in Brazil, Canada and Malaysia (Sarawak), and Indonesia (Irian Jaya),

VIII. Ethnic conflict

(a) The explosion of ethnic, sectarian, inter-communal and tribal conflicts, as in the USSR, Romania, Yugoslavia and Iraq, because of the Kurdish problem and in northern provinces of India threatening the unity of these countries, and also in Liberia, Burma, Somalia, Yugoslavia, South Africa, Burundi and Rwanda, and the persistence and intensification of certain long-standing conflicts, as in East Timor and Irian Jaya, which for the past 15 and 29 years respectively have been waging a war of independence against Indonesia; in Ethiopia, in Lebanon and in Sudan where the current Islamic fundamentalist military regime has regularly bombed civilian targets in its war against the rebel Sudan Peoples' Liberation Army, detained reportedly more political prisoners than any other country in Africa during the past year, and cut off food to civilians in many areas, with up to 11 million people now at risk of starvation in Sudan; in Syria where 4000 Jews still live in three ghettos, deprived of basic rights and unable to leave Syria,

IX. Religious freedom

(a) The prevention of freedom of worship by the state in many countries and the persecution of religious leaders;

POSITIVE DEVELOPMENTS

13. Draws attention to the following *positive* developments which took place during the period under review:

I. Elections and progress towards pluralism

(a) The emergence of elected governments in Eastern and Central Europe where during 1990 in the space of four months six Warsaw Pact countries which had suffered from single-party domination for longer than four decades, became free to vote for governments of their choice,

(b) Moves in many African countries towards greater pluralism, prompted partly by the changes in Europe and by the political and economic failure and corruption and oppression of their governments,

(c) Similar pressures in certain Asian countries, with, however, the continuation of authoritarian governments, despite popular pressure in Myanmar (Burma), Thailand, South Korea and China,

(d) The consolidation of the democratic process throughout Latin America, with free and secret elections taking place in Chile, Nicaragua and Haiti, leaving only Cuba under single-party rule, though democracy remained extremely fragile in many countries, such as Peru and Colombia,

(e) In South Africa important steps towards the abolition of apartheid and discussions being held between all the interested parties,

(f) In Western Sahara, the peace plan devised by the UN and accepted by the different parties, but whose implementation is likely to be jeopardized by the Moroccan army's incursions into Western Sahara;

II. Widening spread of information

(a) The spread of the information revolution which has meant that, with the exception of certain very closed societies and states (North Korea, parts of China, Burma for example) information about human rights abuses can be transmitted around the country and outside the country; furthermore, the spread of the idea of the need for all countries to respect human rights, international measures condemning violations and the pressure of public opinion, where possible, and the improved dissemination of information in this sector have all helped and will continue to help to reduce the number of human rights abuses,

III. Growth of the human rights movement

(a) The continuing growth which has taken place throughout the 1980s of associations dedicated to monitoring or promoting respect for human rights, as in Latin America and in such African countries as Burkina Faso, Cameroon, Ivory Coast, Kenya, Mali, Mauritania, Nigeria, Senegal and Uganda,

(b) The establishment by governments of official bodies to respond to complaints of human rights violations, for instance in Benin, Uganda, Zaire, Morocco, Togo, Mexico, Chile, Argentina, Turkey — although some of them have only just started their activities and are not always given adequate support;

(c) The work carried out by the UN Commission on Human Rights and by some regional organisations (such as the OAS) which help to publicise human rights violations committed in many countries,

IV. Conflict resolution

(a) The achievement or the prospect of achievement of a settlement in certain long-standing international conflicts which had long remained unsolved, as in Namibia, Nicaragua, El Salvador, Cambodia, Angola and the Western Sahara, where the referendum on independence for the Saharawi people will soon be held, and a partial settling of the ethnic conflicts in South Africa: in a number of these cases the new entente between the United States and the Soviet Union has undoubtedly played a positive role,

V. Release of political prisoners

(a) The release of numbers of political prisoners in certain countries in the period under review including Zambia (July 1990), Uganda

(April 1990), Burkina Faso (August 1989), South Africa (1989 and 1990), Jordan (September 1989), Benin (August 1989), and Ethiopia, where the three grandsons of former Ethiopian Emperor, Haile Selassie, were released in September 1989 after 15 years of detention without trial;

REGIONAL SYSTEMS OF HUMAN RIGHTS PROTECTION

14. Reaffirms its belief that regional forms of human rights protection, as under the European Convention on Human Rights and under the Organisation of American States Charter might be more effective than other wider-ranging international instruments, but only if they were provided with monitoring systems and possible sanctions to be applied in the event of violations, which they are not at present;

15. Calls upon those Community countries which have not yet done so to:
— remove the death penalty from their statute-books (Greece, Belgium, Italy, Spain and the United Kingdom) as it has been abolished in practice;
— ratify Protocol No. 6 to the European Convention on Human Rights and the Second Optional Protocol to the International Covenant on Civil and Political Rights,
— ratify the European Convention for the prevention of torture;

16. Hopes that the African Commission on Human and Peoples' Rights, the OAU monitoring body under the African Charter on Human and Peoples' Rights, which now has a permanent headquarters, will enjoy an enhanced role as a result of the changes taking place in Africa and will be supported in its work by African governments;

17. Regrets that organisations of this kind remain only embryonic in Asia, and that efforts to establish such bodies in the Arab world have been impeded by governments, despite the continuing efforts of the Arab Lawyers' Union, and the Arab Organisation of Human Rights;

18. Notes that throughout the world during the period under review there was a burgeoning of human rights organisations pressing for developments of this kind, with this most significant growth occurring in Eastern and Central Europe, Asia and Africa; and that

the progress of such organisations has continued in Latin America, contributing significantly to the promotion of human rights, standard-setting and the investigation of past violations;

19. Believes that the provisions in the Lomé IV agreement concerned with human rights represent significant progress and hopes that this will lead to increased responsiveness on the part of ACP governments to expressions of concern and representations by the Community about human rights problems;

20. Believes that a fundamental question with major human rights implications is devising ways to enable most of the world's population comprising diverse groups of peoples in the same countries to come together under common political structures, notably in Africa and in the Soviet Union where the problem has emerged dramatically in the period under review;

21. Considers that the new democracies in Central and Eastern Europe which have replaced the previous regimes must be helped, since the persistence of difficult economic situations, which are the cause of discontent among the people, cannot bring about the state of social peace which is needed for these countries on the threshold of democracy to really make up the distance separating them from the Western countries and give their inhabitants a good quality of life;

22. Notes that now that the East/West opposition has come to an end, a new North/South opposition has emerged during the period under review, with a 'poverty curtain' separating the developed and the developing worlds, and notes by way of example that the real income of the average African has declined in real terms over the last 20 years and that the countries of Africa now have international debts equal to the continent's entire GNP at a time when aid from the developed world is falling, recognising that unless this trend is reversed new democracies are very likely to be overwhelmed by economic crises;

23. Believes that although the Commission has proposed to Council (October 1990) the cancellation of ACP debts to the EC (such as special loans, transfers and the rescheduling of special credits) that considerably more initiatives of this kind could be taken;

24. Believes that it is impossible to separate development efforts from the efforts needed to establish democratic states;

25. Recognises that respect for all human rights (political, economic and social) will have to be a key criterion in the evaluation of development policies in the 1990s;

COMMUNITY POLICY

26. Believes that during the period under review there has been a significant evolution in Community thinking about human rights policy, partly prompted by the changes which have taken place in Eastern and Central Europe and by the pressure in other regions of the world towards greater pluralism;

27. Welcomes any moves towards development of a more coherent Community policy on human rights with respect to third countries, and calls on the Commission and Council to ensure that in moving away from a 'selective', 'ad hoc' policy that there is a consistency of approach;

28. Considers that in the role which the Community wishes to play in the peace process in the Middle East the human rights situation in the various Arab states must be involved specifically, in particular where the principles of a constitutional state, democracy, protection of human integrity and freedom of worship are concerned;

29. Notes in this connection that there are many examples in the period under review and subsequently where it is clear that Community policy has been dictated less by human rights considerations than by other interests as, for instance, in policy towards Myanmar (Burma), China, Syria and Morocco among others;

30. Welcomes the objective of inserting references to common commitments with respect to human rights into a growing number of Community agreements with third countries or groups of countries, as in the Lomé IV agreement, the agreement between the Community and the countries party to the General Treaty on Central American Economic Integration, with Argentina, Chile, Mexico and in the Association Agreements currently being negotiated with Poland, Czechoslovakia and Hungary;

31. Calls on the Commission and Council to press for the inclusion of such references in a standard form in the whole range of such agreements concluded by the Community;

32. Calls on the Commission and Council to ensure that in instances where programmable aid is suspended on human rights grounds (as with the Sudan in 1990), this should not lead to any diminution of humanitarian aid or other forms of aid or cooperation which are of direct help to the local population, though great care should be taken to ensure that such aid reaches the people for whom it is intended;

33. Considers that any decision to suspend aid should not be taken merely at the administrative or executive level, but should always be subject to transparent and thorough political deliberation;

34. Calls on European Political Cooperation to be more explicit about criteria used to take up individual cases;

35. Notes that the human rights component of the Helsinki process has expanded considerably, with many important human rights affirmed in the June 1990 Copenhagen document, including minority rights and the right to representative government;

36. Calls on the Commission and Council to ensure that human rights considerations are one of the main pillars in the 'new European architecture' and notes the stress laid on respect for human rights at the November 1990 CSCE summit in Paris, that much of the follow-up activity scheduled to take place before the next full Review Conference in Helsinki in 1992 concerns human rights and that a main commitment in the Final Declaration at the Copenhagen 'human dimension' conference in June 1990 was the creation of a common legal space;

37. Believes that as is the case with the Commission, Parliament should be represented at all appropriate interim meetings (such as the 'human dimension' conference in Moscow in September 1991), as well as at the full review conferences, and records its appreciation of the assistance provided in the past by European Political Cooperation to delegations of Parliament which have attended such CSCE conferences;

38. Believes, in view of the role the Community must play in CSCE, that it is no longer appropriate for the Community as such not to be a signatory to the European Convention on Human Rights, and calls on the Council, without further delay, to respond positively to the Commission's proposal to the Council in November 1990 for

Community accession to the European Convention, and for the Commission to be given a negotiating mandate to that end;

39. Notes that whereas all legal acts of the Member States are subject to human rights control by the Strasbourg Commission and Human Rights Court, EC acts are not subject to this mechanism and thus its institutions benefit from a sort of 'immunity' from scrutiny to the detriment of the citizens' protection system;

40. Notes further that because of the growing scope of the Community's competences in economic and other areas, Community legislation has come to have increasing human rights implications, for instance, draft directives on the retention of personal data and on the right of residence;

41. Believes that these considerations are of particular importance in view of the proposals before the Intergovernmental conference on European citizenship and recalls the document by the Twelve published in December 1990, before the intergovernmental conference started, stating that the great majority of delegations agreed that the concept of European citizenship should form part of the new Treaty, together with a number of specific rights to be defined at the conference in the areas of civil rights, economic and social rights, equality of treatment with regard to social legislation and diplomatic protection in third countries;

42. Calls for the Intergovernmental Conference and other meetings reviewing the provisions of European Political Cooperation and the Community's external relations policy, to state explicitly that concern for human rights is one of the cornerstones of Community foreign policy;

43. Calls on the Foreign Ministers meeting in European Political Cooperation to draw up an annual report on human rights worldwide for the European Parliament;

44. Calls on the Council and the Member States to give further consideration to drawing up a European Bill of Rights and for the concept of European citizenship to be enshrined in the future Treaty by means of a series of rights guaranteed by adequate political and legal mechanisms, and furthermore that the Community should be given responsibility for controls over immigration and asylum;

45. Calls on Community Member States to review national

legislation or administrative rulings to prevent the export of specialised equipment, ostensibly for 'security purposes', which can be abused by repressive governments, and not to cooperate with such governments in providing training or information about interrogation techniques;

46. Calls for the development of more structured cooperation between Parliament and the Commission on human rights, partly through an inter-institutional working party (as proposed in the previous annual report), and partly through periodic meetings at an appropriate level, where European Political Cooperation could be represented to discuss priorities for action in the field of human rights and to prepare Community positions at such international fora such as CSCE and the United Nations;

47. Calls on the Commission to examine the possibility of making one of its members specifically responsible for questions concerning human rights and citizens' rights and to provide him with the assistance of a specialist task force;

48. Requests that explicit reference be made to human rights objectives in the annual presentation of the Commission's programme;

49. Calls for similar meetings in the budgetary field between representatives of Parliament and the Commission to ensure greater transparency with regard to human rights-related spending and better coordination to ensure that funds are targeted within a balanced global perspective, and there is better coordination and balance between different budget headings;

50. Calls for an increase in the funds available for human rights-related activities and programmes in different parts of the world which should also make provision for the technical means and staff to implement them, in view of the extremely limited resources of the Commission in the human rights field;

51. Calls for more channelling of funds towards regional human rights organisations, in an even-handed, geographically balanced way;

52. Calls for a significant part of the European Community's human rights budget to go to education and training, as part of a rolling pluri-annual programme, to enable lawyers, doctors, civil servants,

prison personnel, police and members of other professions to serve in departments concerned with human rights in Member States and in the Commission and Parliament, which should also initiate specific human rights 'traineeships' of three months or more, modelled on the *stagiaire* programme;

53. Wishes the European Foundation for Human Rights in Amsterdam, which is financed by the Community, to be more closely integrated into the Community's activities with definite objectives and the involvement of the European Parliament;

UNITED NATIONS

54. Deeply regrets that only about half of the UN member states have ratified the United Nations agreements on human rights, that only one state in five could be said to respect those covenants and calls upon those Community countries which have not ratified the International Covenant on Civil and Political Rights, and its two optional protocols, the International Covenant on Economic, Social and Cultural Rights and the Convention against torture, to do so, while at the same time recognising with regret that ratification in itself is no indication of compliance;

55. Welcomes the improved coordination among the Twelve at the United Nations, where at the beginning of the 1990 session of the UN Commission on Human Rights, the President-in-Office delivered a decisive statement on behalf of the Twelve, and there was also a statement on behalf of the Twelve on the human rights situation in certain countries of particular concern;

56. Notes that at the May 1990 session of the UN Economic and Social Council the Irish presidency played a key role in resolving the difficult problem of agreeing an enlargement of the membership of the Commission on Human Rights as well as on measures to enhance the effectiveness of the Commission;

57. Calls on the Twelve to continue to work to improve and make more effective UN human rights activities;

58. Believes that the European Community has not sufficiently developed its links with the human rights structures of the Council of Europe or with the United Nations or its specialised agencies, and believes that there should be careful consideration of whether

the Community could at least be granted observer status with, for instance, certain bodies such as the UNHCR;

59. Reaffirms its belief that the United Nations is the world's pre-eminent standard-setting human rights organisation and also believes that the rules of procedure of the Security Council must be amended, as they are based on outmoded criteria resulting from the Second World War which should therefore be reformulated;

60. Reiterates its concern that at the UN, particularly the Commission on Human Rights, regional alliances have too often prevented condemnation of countries where human rights abuses were manifest and that this politicisation and unprincipled alliances remain a feature of the human rights work of the United Nations;

ACTIVITIES OF PARLIAMENT

61. Reaffirms the undertakings made in previous annual reports and its belief that Parliament, through its links with political forces in third countries, and as the world's only international elected Parliament, has an active role to play in promoting respect for human rights, and that this corresponds to the wishes of millions of Community citizens and could not be considered *ultra vires* or as interference in the internal affairs of third countries;

62. Undertakes to make greater use of Parliament's formal and informal means to take action in favour of human rights concerns to representatives of third countries;

63. Considers that beyond public pronouncement, the Parliament will not be able to adopt a more active and effective role and will lose its credibility unless its own internal structures within the Secretariat and its voting procedure in plenary sittings are not significantly improved and strengthened and notes that despite the efforts made in that direction in recent years, the growing number of appeals to the European Parliament and the demonstrable successes in this field call for effective improvements; considers further that the European Parliament should be guaranteed the possibility of being informed of all violations of human rights occurring in the world so that it may, with the authority it has acquired in recent years, intervene where necessary on the basis of definite and indisputable information;

64. Decides to pursue greater coordination with other national and

international bodies concerned with human rights, both within and outside the European Community, as well as with the Commission and European Political Cooperation;

65. Calls on the Commission and on the President-in-Office of the Foreign Ministers meeting in European Political Cooperation (in accordance with paragraph 7(2) of the Decision of 28 February 1986), formally to submit observations on this resolution;

66. Instructs its President to forward this resolution to the Commission, the Council, the Foreign Ministers meeting in European Political Cooperation, the Council of Europe, the Secretary-General of the United Nations and the governments of all the countries mentioned in this motion for a resolution.